Use All the Crayons!

This Book Is Free

That's right. Free. Anyone who wants a copy mailed to his or her home, no charge, is welcome to one. Just ask.

Author Chris Rodell, of course, encourages you to buy it and hopes you'll support him and the people who distribute, promote, and sell books. But if you're one of those Americans who are out of work and having a tough time, or if you know a US serviceman or woman who might benefit from a book that aims to brighten daily lives, then Rodell wants you to get in touch at storyteller@chrisrodell.com.

He doesn't believe a book that, at its heart, aims to help people be happy should be withheld from anyone over a few dollars. "It's said the best things in life—love, friendship, laughter—are free," Rodell says. "I don't presume that this book is one of the best things in life but, by God, there's nothing to say it can't keep good company."

Use All the Crayons!

The Colorful Guide
to
Simple Human Happiness

CHRIS RODELL

www.EightDaysToAmish.com

iUniverse LLC
Bloomington

Use All the Crayons!
The Colorful Guide to Simple Human Happiness

iUniverse books may be ordered through booksellers or by contacting:

iUniverse
1663 Liberty Drive
Bloomington, IN 47403
www.iuniverse.com
1-800-Authors (1-800-288-4677)

ISBN: 978-1-9389-0850-7 (sc)
ISBN: 978-1-9389-0851-4 (e)

Library of Congress Control Number: 2013917557

Printed in the United States of America

iUniverse rev. date: 10/7/2013

To Josie and Lucy

Foreword

One of my neighbors in Latrobe, Pennsylvania, Chris Rodell, has dropped into my office from time to time over the last decade or so to conduct a variety of friendly interviews and, once a year, to drop off some copies of his golf desk calendar with its daily gems that I often find informative and frequently amusing. Many of his interviews have wound up on our ArnoldPalmer.com website or in our publication, *Kingdom Magazine*.

I thought I had gotten to know Chris fairly well from those many visits, but I really hadn't realized the true extent of his literary talents until I had a chance to see a draft of his latest book. *Use All the Crayons!* is an interesting and amusing trip through precisely 501 wide-ranging tips on life surrounding thirty-three short essays that are thoughtful and insightful.

Who would have thought to wonder what would happen to a traveling knight in shining armor when he showed up at airport security? Or suggest that, while standing on a busy street corner, you scream into your cell phone: "No! No! No! The incision should be made behind the left ear!"

That's the sort of fun reading you will find in these pages, taking you to Tip No. 501—Learn the fine art of knowing precisely when to quit. I think you will enjoy what appears on all the pages that lead to that fitting conclusion.

—Arnold Palmer

Preface

Self-help authors offer an endless supply of books aimed at making you, the reader, a happier and more well-rounded individual. If you've bought these books and they've fulfilled all they promised, we're sorry because people tend to be suspicious of happy people. They think they're up to something. Bailed-out bankers tend to be happy. Anyone alert enough to pay attention to the news ends up figuring that happiness, at least on this planet, must be an unnatural state of mind. How can anybody be happy when so many of our fellow men and women are miserable.

This book doesn't promise to make you happy, but it'll make you more fun and more interesting—more colorful. A healthy and aware happiness is bound to ensue. Happy people, you see, aren't necessarily colorful, but colorful people are universally happy. People resent happy people. They invite colorful people to all the coolest parties.

I've never had a lot of money. In fact, for many, many years, my idea of a splurge has been to order a pizza with pepperoni *and* sausage. But since kindergarten, I've never lacked for friends, laughs, or love. I'm no smarter than most, less ambitious than all but a handful, and I'm freighted with a God-given laziness that has stifled any natural abilities others would have successfully exploited to their prosperous advantage.

About five years ago, just as America began hitting a historic rough patch, it began to dawn on me that things weren't working out so well for me either. I was constantly broke. Anticipated breakthroughs never materialized. I'd once been considered a promising young writer. With my forty-fifth birthday behind me, I was no longer young, and any promise seemed to have vanished.

That was all a bit surprising to an optimist like me. But what was even more surprising was how pleased I was with my joyful little life. I was happy. I had a lovely wife and two beautiful daughters.

We had a host of dedicated friends and seemed to attract squads of lively new ones with carefree frequency. Each day was filled with laughter and fun.

As a freelance writer, I'd awoken unemployed for the past twenty years with a natural obligation to find something fun or lucrative to do. I was paid meager sums to write scattered features and occasional essays for magazines like *Esquire, Sports Illustrated, Men's Health, Golf,* and other top magazines. It sounds prestigious, but the reality is I haven't earned more than $21,700 during the last four years—and just a bit more than half that in the lampblack days of 2009. With professional prospects dim, I turned to blogging, the last refuge of the underemployed writer who still believes he has something to say. I called my blog www.EightDaysToAmish.com, a grim nod to the fact that I always seemed like I was a little over a week away from having to do things like churn my own butter and try raising two sassy daughters without things like electricity or gas-powered transportation.

On some days I'd work.

Many days I did not. Neither did my darling wife. She did part-time editing jobs and became one of those maniacal coupon clippers, the tearing din of scissors snipping paper becoming the soundtrack of our evenings.

Like America, we were broke. We'd pilfered most of our savings. We cut back on insurance and health care. Every gauge we'd been conditioned to check said we should have been unhappy, distraught, angry. Yet we were not. For anyone raised to equate income with self-worth, it was a little disorienting.

Money wasn't buying our happiness.

What was?

I decided to make a little list. I jotted down the things that made me laugh or feel soulful. For instance, I'd play precocious little pranks on my unsuspecting wife. She'd recruit our daughters in score-evening schemes. I daydreamed about how the world could be a better place—*fax leftovers to the starving* (see no. 334)!—and I wrote down what I thought. The little list began to grow.

You're holding the result in your hands.

We, as a nation, remain mired in the midst of a historically difficult time. Many of us are out of work or underemployed. Yet, some of us continue to steadfastly confound the pollsters by saying we've never felt more optimistic about our shared futures. We believe we've survived the worst and our best days still lie ahead.

Maybe we're simultaneously discovering that the excesses of the past decades weren't what mattered. It's all the little moments of mortar between the big ones that do. Here are five hundred tips that will give your day a little jolt of joy. Feel free to work the suggestions into your world and add your own.

Rich or poor, it's up to each of us to color our lives as we see fit. We can sketch them out in uniformly dark colors or we can use all the crayons.

It's up to you.

I hope to see you at the party.

Introduction

Charcoal and lampblack: those were the only two colors the company that would grow to be Crayola Crayons produced when it was founded in 1864. And it took good lighting and a discerning eye to differentiate between the two. Today, the children who use Crayola products can choose from more than 120 different colors, including Azure, Laser Lemon, and Razzmatazz. What child isn't glad to be alive in such a vibrant age? The company, which now earns more than $100 million each year, says the average child will wear down more than 730 crayons before he or she turns ten years old.

Like a box of crayons, we are all born with an astounding range of color options, from Mauvelous to Tickle Me Pink. We can paint our lives as brightly or dimly as we choose—but through life, some of us lose or wear down some of our more dazzling colors, living each and every day as if it were either charcoal or lampblack.

It doesn't have to be that way. Nor should it. *Use All the Crayons!* is your uplifting, humorous, spiritual guidebook about how to make every day as vivacious as Atomic Tangerine to illuminate even your most lampblack days.

Reading Instructions

This book avoids chronological construction that may have helped ease confusion. Flow is random, logic evasive.

Each item, whether historical, current, or futuristic, took about thirty seconds to type. By that narrow calculation, the book you're holding took about four hours and seventeen minutes to compose. My recollections suggest it took a good bit longer.

Once typed, I didn't deign to put any of the items in any mystical order; there are no hidden codes that once deciphered lead to greater intellectual or materialistic treasures. It is what it is.

Persons referred to in the text may on one page be eight years old and then on a later page travel back to when they were just four. At some parts, the stories suggest my office is in a basement, and in others it is above a friendly tavern. Do not let the change of location inebriate your mental equilibrium. It doesn't matter. It is helpful, but not necessary, to read first the items preceding the Colorful Days Diary extrapolations and treat both the way polite people treat an introduction to a married couple; that means being simultaneously attentive to both.

Other than that one suggestion, the book is nimble in its options for any readers eager to engage it. It can be read the traditional way or in reverse. You can open pages at random or create some numerical-based routine—spend one reading session perusing only the items divisible by seven—understood only by you. Or you can start at the last page and go in reverse.

The book is not a mystery. There's no surprise ending. The butler didn't do it. Backwards or forwards, either way really isn't that important. I think the best way to explore what follows is with an open mind, a playful heart, and without any ambition that any of it is ever going to make perfect sense.

Sort of like life.

1. Make time for the important things—and consult a nearby five-year-old anytime you forget what's important.

Colorful Days Diary

Resignation mingled with euphoria when I heard my daughter describe to her friends just what her daddy does for a living. She and her little trio of chums were busily cluttering the kitchen table with colorful scraps of construction paper while I was cluttering the nearby countertop with discarded wheat bread crusts that would have rendered peanut butter and jelly sandwiches inedible to the quartet of five-year-olds.

It's a conversation all children get around to, and I was standing right there when the little redheaded neighbor girl brought it up.

"What's your daddy do? Mine helps sick people," she said with estimable pride.

They went right around in a little circle.

"Mine fixes cars."

"He builds homes."

Then, in a matter-of-fact voice, my beloved daughter drove a stake through any remaining ambitions I'd nurtured that one day I might achieve something notable in my profession. What does her daddy do?

"He plays with me."

My first thought was, Man, that's not going to look good on the loan applications.

I should have seen it coming. For the past few years, the dawning day would greet me with the very same challenge: achieve or enjoy?

During that time, the record was clear: if I chose to enjoy, I succeeded every time.

I'd go golfing, fish, picnic with the family, and revel in the simple joys of being a father. That meant I'd drop whatever I was doing the instant my daughter marched down the stairs into my basement office with her Barbie dolls and said, "Daddy, let's play," with a voice that left no room for artful refusal.

There are few things more entertaining than fully engaging a wound-up five-year-old at play. In my basement office where I earn my living writing stories about unusual events for offbeat news sources ("Town Saved by Giant Ball of Twine!" ... "What People Named Pat Downs Think about Airport Pat-Downs"), I've seen things too amazing for jaded editors to believe. For instance, I've seen my daughter fly. I've seen her slay dragons. I've seen her carry on intelligent conversations with the dog and even laugh at his stupid jokes—and that dog's not funny.

It's an unstructured jolliness that begins to slip from the grasp of children even one year later, an age when chalk-wielding adults first begin imposing conformity on classrooms of fidgety kids.

On the other hand, my record of achievements is skimpy. I've toiled at my profession, contributed meager amounts to worthy charities, and have built nothing that will endure beyond my mortal years.

That's the kind of self-assessment that ought to depress someone who, like most wage-earning adults, was born with a kernel of ambition that's been culturally nurtured to burst like Jack's beanstalk clear to the clouds. By middle age, we're all on a uniform march to do better, earn more, and build a legacy that others will admire.

Not me. Not since the day I read a prominent obituary about the passing of a man who'd certainly awakened nearly every day and opted to achieve. And he did. He did in ways that will forever enrich mankind.

That great man had developed multiple vaccinations that literally saved the lives of millions of people. Who knows? Perhaps even mine.

Yet, I'd never once heard his name. Through a selfless life of enduring professional victories, that man of greatness had never achieved the kind of notoriety that would land him a significant mention in the newspapers until he passed away.

Worse, I forgot his name by the time I got to the sports pages and immersed myself in the fine-print box scores that detailed how my fantasy league baseball team fared the night before.

That's the way it is with the deaths of prominent poets, soldiers, and statesmen. Men and women of true greatness are forgotten with the turn of a page. The most they can hope for is that their life's work will endure long enough to bore eighth-grade history students twenty-five years after they're gone.

Who among us will be remembered by anyone other than our loved ones twenty-five years after our passing? Fifty years? One hundred?

Humanitarian rock god Bono—and is there a cooler job description in the world?—recently remarked that the music he makes with the band U2 will not be forgotten in one hundred years. (He's wrong. I love U2, but the churning pop culture will render their music irrelevant twenty-five tidy years after Bono's demise.)

The odds of us accomplishing anything are long and stacked against us. That ought not to depress.

It ought to liberate.

A test: ask ten people, "Hey, how've you been?" Ten will likely respond with some variation of, "Man, I've been busy," as if to be otherwise somehow violates the very laws of nature.

If that's the case, then consider me an outlaw in every sense of the word. See, I'm a wanted man.

Just ask my daughter.

That's her I hear marching down the stairs. She has her Barbie dolls. That means it's time for me to, for now, end this silly little diversion. It's time to shut the lid on the laptop, to disengage my brain from striving for coherent thoughts and structured sentences.

It's time for me to get back to work.

2. Learn to say "Thank you!" in three different languages. Example: *"Yakoke!"* means "Thank you!" in Choctaw; *"Arigato!"* in Japanese; and *"Efcharisto!"* in Greek. Remember, always say it with a smile.

3. Write a letter to a TV star who was popular when you were a kid but hasn't done anything lately. Explain how much the actor's character meant to you. You'll probably get a letter back and may have an exciting new pen pal.

4. Make up a risqué toast you can use at parties to liven things up and draw some flattering attention your way. Or use this old Irish gem: "May you be found dead in bed at the age of ninety—shot—victim of a jealous lover."

5. Plan a dream vacation using colorful brochures and an itinerary of places to stay and things to do. Put them in a large envelope in a secure place. Mark the envelope, "Things to do the day after I win the lottery."

6. Get a $75 tattoo of an $18,000 Rolex for your left wrist (see No. 310).

7. When people do something uncommonly considerate, thank them. Then send an urgent letter or e-mail insisting they call their parents right away to congratulate them for having done such a fine job of raising an outstanding human being.

8. Buy an expensive belt, pair of shoes, or other accessory. The cost may make you gulp, but it's a one-time purchase that will likely last you the rest of your life. You'll feel good about yourself every time you wear it, and friends and strangers alike will respect you for having impeccable taste.

9. Ask a brainy 6 year old to spell "rule." Listen, then say, "You know my name's not Ellie. Now spell rule." Repeat.

10. In the wee hours of the night, superglue a quarter to the sidewalk outside of a busy downtown office building. Then pack a lunch and spend the noon hour watching frustrated executives try to surreptitiously pick it up.

11. Colorful conversation starter: tell people that in 1968 when the Rolling Stones released "Jumpin' Jack Flash," gas, gas, gas was thirty-three cents a gallon, gallon, gallon.

12. Add your own spices, but the five main ingredients for any loving relationship are these: play, tickle, cuddle, kiss, hug.

13. Spend a thoughtful Sunday morning in church, listening carefully to the sermon. When you get home, write down some honest, soul-searching theological questions about the lesson and make an appointment to discuss them with the preacher.

14. Learn how to tie a balloon into the shape of a simple little horse. Then be sure to carry some slim balloons to the next party or family gathering where children will be present.

15. Try to conform to expert recommendations by getting eight hours of sleep a night. Then, just to be safe, get another hour or two when the sun is up.

Colorful Days Diary

Many fine Americans are eager to stand up and fight against perceived flaws they believe are harming the nation.

Me, I'm about to lie down and nap over one.

The stigma against sleep is costing America. No one is getting enough of it. That's obvious in our stress, our productivity, and our spiraling ethics.

Well-rested people aren't prone to violence, sloth, or felonious business practices.

We should be inviting sleep, not fighting it. If sleep beckons, we should obey, the exception being people like train conductors and airline pilots.

We've all heard hyper-productive type-A busybodies brag about needing just four hours of sleep per night, but you never hear anyone bragging about enjoying ten hours of sleep each night.

My nights are interrupted by two tiny sleep bandits, miscellaneous woodsy creature noises, and the nervous yipping of a dog with a BB-sized bladder capacity.

I'm on a quest to get everybody under my roof to go to bed two hours earlier and get up two hours later.

The kids would be asleep by eight and would wake up at nine. Sure, my daughter would miss her first hour of fourth grade, but nothing important happens in school until ten—and I don't mean 10:00 a.m.

I mean tenth grade.

My wife and I would be under the covers by 9:30 p.m. and up at 8:30 a.m.

Doesn't that sleep schedule strike you as nirvana?

It does me.

Not my wife. She got mad at me recently for dozing off at 9:30 after reading to one of the kids and, ahh, just staying there in our bed like a sedated mental patient clear through the next morning.

For the first time in months, I reached the most hallowed state of sleep. Yes, I hit pillow-puddlin' slobber sleep.

In sleep terms, that's like bowling a 300.

To her, it seemed like a waste of time. She thinks we should stay awake so long that we become actual zombies so we can enjoy adult shows about things like fictional zombies.

In an ideal world—and in any ideal world, there are no children—we'd have about an hour of bedtime unwinding, reading, TV watching, or couple cuddlin' from 9:00 to 10:00 p.m. each and every night.

But years ago, we made the cheapskate mistake of not getting a DVR for our bedroom.

Without the bedroom DVR, we are forced to stay awake in the living room long enough to execute a series of maneuvers similar to what happens in far-flung US Army outposts around the globe.

We need to secure the fireplace, check the perimeter, and do a quick head count before finally getting to bed at eleven sharp in time to watch a 1996 episode of *Seinfeld* we've only seen 114 times before.

It's so bad it took us four nights to watch one two-hour, forty-five-minute movie. We'd recorded the outstanding 1959 Alfred Hitchcock movie, *Anatomy of a Murder*, starring Jimmy Stewart.

We both kept falling asleep during key segments and then spent breakfast trying to unravel plot lines and determine if we'd spied the Hitchcock cameo he so cleverly inserted into each of his films.

It wasn't until the movie finally concluded that we realized it would have been Hitchcock's most clever cameo ever.

Because in our sleep-deprived state, neither of us ever realized it was an Otto Preminger movie.

Everything would improve if we got more sleep.

Our families would have less time to bicker. We'd all get more done in less time.

Me, I'd have time to dream up better story ideas and, thus, would start receiving a better class of rejection letters from more prominent sleep-deprived editors.

Sleeplessness is often confused with physical virtuosity. It's a quality we've always sought in our elected leaders and a keystone critique of those who every four years spend the frosty months tromping around desolate Iowa.

It should be the other way around.

So wake up, America!

And go right back to bed.

We'll all be better off.

From sea to shining *zzzzzzzzz* ...

16. Learn to juggle three beanbags. It'll take you a persistent month or so's worth of bending over, but the reward will be a lifetime of show-offy enjoyment.

17. Buy a carton of your spouse's favorite expensive ice cream, make a big presentation of it, and share a sample bite. Then, before your spouse can enjoy a real splurge, secretly consume the entire contents and place the empty box prominently inside the freezer. Watch for the outraged reaction. Better have a full spare hidden behind the frozen dinners, though.

18. Ask a 6 year old what God looks like. Then ask if God rides a bike.

19. Whenever you finish a roll of toilet paper, blow through the cardboard roll like it's a trumpet. The announcement will let everyone know it's time to shop for more TP.

20. Unplug the TV for one week. Studies show that 70 percent of parents who watch fewer than six hours of television per week (a fraction of the national average of twenty-eight hours), report their kids have fewer fights. Those same people report by a whopping 99 percent that they are generally happy and satisfied with their home life. Next time, unplug it for two weeks.

21. Invent a heroic figure from your family tree and inspire your youngster with bold tales of ancestral adventures fighting evildoers down through history. Have this ancestor serve under important generals, rescue damsels in distress, or slay dragons on behalf of fair maidens. It may be untrue, but it'll take some of the pressure off you to be so historically heroic.

22. Keep a stack of useless papers by your desk at home in case your child comes in and wants to play. Make a big show of tearing the papers in half and tossing them into the trash, telling your child, "Your time's more important to me than anything the boss needs me to get done. Let's go play!"

23. Learn to whittle a blunt stick into something sharp. It's a great way to clear your head of stressful thoughts and allow creativity to seep in. Tell anyone who asks why you're doing it that you're trying to think of anything as contradictorily pointless as whittling.

24. Colorful conversation starter: ask astronomer friends if light years are less filling than regular years.

25. Make a family outing of going to a movie. Before the previews end, ask your spouse to run out and get some popcorn. While your partner's gone, move the entire family to a distant part of the theater and swear them to silence. It'll be a great bonding experience as you all watch your loved one helplessly prowling about the darkened theater in a vain search for lost loved ones.

26. Tell parents that you intend to home school your child for purely selfish reasons. Tell them that you want junior to be a doctor and that the chance of getting into a really good medical school will be better if you fill out a transcript that says your child was a great student, played well with others, and kept his room really, really clean.

27. Make sure you make the special occasions special. And make sure when someone shares special news with you, you treat it as something special.

Colorful Days Diary

I was privileged to take part in a sacred ceremony last night. A friend of mine told me that he and his wife are having a baby. Their first.

I was the first person outside of his parents he'd told.

He's a former student of mine, and it's fair to say I'm a sort of a mentor to him. He tells me he'd like to be just like me.

And he's not at all referring to frequent episodes of drunken revelry, ample hammock time, and an apparent ability to skate through life with no visible means of support.

He wants to be a writer like me.

I have trouble wrapping my head around that ambition. Two years ago, he heard me for thirteen weeks profess what a failure I consider my career.

I've written for many prominent magazines—once or twice. I wake up nearly every night troubled by my inability to earn money.

The stack of rejection letters my most cherished book projects have drawn are now thicker than the books themselves.

I'm flattered he thinks I'm such a great writer because he, indeed, is a great writer. He's already written many important stories for prestigious magazines.

So he may never write like me.

To write like me, I tell him, you need to become seasoned by decades of failure.

I think what he admires most about me, and this is admirable, is I'll never quit.

We get together for beers in Pittsburgh maybe once every six months or so to talk career. He gives me bona fide contacts to top magazines he's sure will be interested in running my stories, and I tell him about my latest career humiliation.

When I say what he told me is sacred, I mean that. It happens in a bar, not a church. It is consecrated not with sacramental wines, but with intoxicating spirits.

It's not the kind of thing you tell your buddies right away. I don't know any guys that run out in the street to scream their wives are having a baby—not unless they want to get run over by a bus.

You don't want to tell a common moron who'll blurt out, "Man, is your life going to change!"

I heard that so often I reflexively began responding, "Well, that's good, because up till now it has really, really sucked!"

You want to tell someone who will reassure you that fatherhood isn't going to lay devastation to your happy young life.

I had to go clear to Florida to find my guy. I was there doing a story about the carnival industry.

He was a perfect stranger and one of the reasons I'll always sit next to strangers in bars I've never been to. He was a big guy, kind of quiet, but looked capable of making a lot of noise if things got rough.

We hardly said a word to each other for an hour. We just sat there sipping beer and watching the baseball game.

Then it became a guy's version of speed dating: Where you from? What do you do? You golf? My grass needs cut. The bartenders are all cool here. Yeah, I hate the Red Sox, too.

He smiled sunshine when he mentioned he had two little girls. About an hour later, we were new best friends and I said, "You know, you're the first guy I've told, but I found out last week I'm going to be a dad."

It was like I blasted him with happy lightning.

He told me that the moment I held my new child would be the happiest day of my life and every day would get better after that. He told me that bedtime stories would become the highlight of my day. He told me that nothing I achieved in my career would make me as happy as waking up every day knowing I am a father.

And he told me a lie.

He said he was a landscaper.

He was a prophet.

I said good-bye to Matt and said a parking lot prayer that he achieves all his ambitions and becomes just like me.

A happy man who happens to write.

28. In the presence of a beloved young grandchild, niece, nephew, or offspring, answer a ringing phone and pretend it's the president of the United States calling to ask your opinion on important world affairs. The unwitting caller will be confused, but the wide-eyed child will be mighty impressed.

29. Keep a deck of cards at your desk or in a convenient place at home. Anytime anyone asks you to do a menial task, offer an alternative and then cut the cards. Low card has to do it twice. Most people can't resist a wager.

30. Stick a Post-it note on the forehead of an infant and watch the baby spend the next twenty minutes playfully trying to swipe it off. Make sure the infant's the offspring of a friend or relative of yours—and snatch the sticky away before chronic cross-eyes sets in.

31. For a really great party that will impress your kids, friends, and neighbors, find a tree with a sturdy fork in

it about twenty feet off the ground. Screw four bolts with eyeholes in at the base of the fork. Then run about thirty feet of medical supply tubing through a pouch and knot the ends into the bolts. Voila! You've just made a giant slingshot!

32. Learn some basic sign language. It's becoming popular for adults to teach all children a smattering of sign language. Doctors agree that children who know basic sign language enjoy verbal and cognitive advantages. For the adults, it's just cool to have a new way of expressing yourself in traffic.

33. Every time you stay in a hotel, take the Gideon's Bible out of the drawer and open it to Luke 12:22. Read it, and then put a five-dollar bill in between those pages and return the book to the drawer. The passage talks about how God always takes care of our needs and how we shouldn't worry. If someone is looking for inspiration, perhaps your five-dollar bill will seem like a divine reminder.

34. Ask security guards manning the airport metal detectors what would happen if a noble knight wearing a suit of armor tried to pass through. Better yet, wear a suit of armor for your next flight.

35. Warn dedicated premed students that if they do nothing but study anatomy they are destined to be real know bodies.

36. Enjoy at least part of a warm summer night outside in the nude and away from the prying eyes of prurient neighbors. Be sure to invite someone you love—and don't forget to bring some bug spray!

37. Smile and make eye contact with strangers on the sidewalk. The passersby may never be in a position to help you, but it lets people know the world's not as unfriendly as the front pages would lead you to believe.

38. If you see someone driving with their right turn signal endlessly blinking, pull alongside them and "signal" the inadvertent error by vigorously blinking your right eye until they recognize the error. Do this without wrecking your vehicle into theirs ... or anyone else's.

39. Wake up every day with the realization that all it takes to succeed in America beyond your wildest dreams is one really good idea. Then spend the rest of the day trying to find one.

40. If you're right handed, then you've probably allowed your left hand to become a loafer. Use the less dominant hand to brush your teeth, pick up a fork, and do other menial tasks you usually do with the dominant hand. Studies show that repeated use of this easy technique helps stimulate the opposite side of the brain.

Colorful Days Diary

The hot water was pouring down over my body as I stood in the shower in deep contemplation about what to use for that day's shampoo.

Should I use a splash of my wife's good stuff? Or should I go with the industrial stuff I use near daily? Or given that I'd be getting my monthly haircut in about an hour, should I just scrub my head with a bar of cheap soap?

So what'd I do?

I grabbed the good stuff and poured out a healthy palm full. I felt honor bound to give the hairs that had served me so well a kind of last meal before I dutifully took them off to their scissored demise.

I wonder how much further along what for lack of a better word I call my "career" would be if I devoted such strategic thinking to my livelihood. I'd doubtless be overscheduled with award dinners and gala parties held on my behalf.

Of course, that would mean I'd be missing multiple reruns of things like *M*A*S*H*, *Seinfeld*, and *Green Acres*, and I have to wonder if it'd be worth it.

I wonder about a lot of things.

For instance, years ago, I began to wonder about my lazy good-for-nothing left hand. It never did a darned thing.

Sure, I'm right handed, but that didn't mean the left hand couldn't, well, lend a hand once in a while. I wouldn't trust it to toss a dart if a pregnant woman was standing within eight feet of the cork, but for sure it could pick up a beer mug once in a while.

Ever since, I've made a concerted effort to drink left handed, to brush my teeth left handed, and to operate the computer mouse with the southerly paw. Think about it. It all makes perfect sense.

If you're brushing your teeth with your right hand exclusively, you're probably neglecting some of the back teeth on your left side. And if you're grinding away with the computer mouse with only your right hand, think about what you're doing to your overall posture—that upraised right arm jittering all over the place while your left side hangs dormant.

I'm convinced that many of the aches and infirmities that afflict the elderly aren't from some long-ago acute injury but rather from the grinding accumulation of daily poor posture and habits we never bother to address.

So, given all my free time devoted to wondering silently about these health issues, I began to proselytize aloud about this sort of wisdom.

It's a fun pastime to see the expressions on people's faces when you suggest to them that, really, for their own good and the good of their teeth, they should switch hands.

Most people will simply try to ignore you. Some will stare at you like slack-jawed sheep. But once in a while, you can actually make an impression.

That happened with one of my regular bartenders—and, yes, feel free to wonder what one person needs with more than one bartender. Sure, he thought I was crazy to devote even a minute to thinking about it, but putting that aside, he saw a kernel of wisdom in the idea.

He was the first guy I thought about a couple of months ago after I'd left an appointment to get a new suit tailored. The tailor was doing his mundane measurements when he abruptly stopped.

"Well, I'll be darned," he said. "That's something you don't see too often."

"Something wrong?"

"Not at all. But your arms are exactly the same length. I measured twice to be sure. Most people have right arms that are much longer if they're right handed, and longer left arms if they're left handed. Yours are exactly the same length."

I dashed straight to the bar to tell Keith, who couldn't have been more effusive in his gushing support.

"Hey, man, it's paying off! That's great! Guess what, everybody—Rodell's arms are both the same length!"

At least I think he was being supportive. It could have been mocking ridicule. I often confuse the two.

But is it paying off? Am I making a difference? Will it matter years from now, when everyone else is walking around lopsided, that I'm pointing straight up? Am I doing something that will be beneficial to my health, or am I just wasting my time thinking about so many possibly trivial matters?

I wonder.

41. Just bending your neck and glancing up at the clouds doesn't count. Lie flat on the ground in a grassy field on a warm spring day and stare at the sky. It is one of the most serene and liberating feelings in the world.

42. Get a practical tattoo. Skin art is passé and doesn't lend color to anyone's life—not unless the ink imparts a message. Get the important dates—anniversaries, birthdays, etc., tattooed on your forearm. That way you'll never forget and

can reference them when purchasing lottery tickets (and won't that make a great story when you win!).

43. Stand in a dimly lit room, press record on your video camera and spin until you're dizzy. Then immediately post and boast you just survived two minutes in the eye of a tornado.

44. Designate one weekend a month "Opposites Weekend," and do the exact opposite of what you normally do. Call different friends, read different newspapers and magazines, think different thoughts.

45. Create a two-year time capsule. We all compile too much unnecessary junk. Every two years, set a day aside and gather three shirts, three photographs, three favorite playlist printouts, three pay stubs from work, and a list of three current goals. Put them all in a box in a remote part of the attic or basement. Two years later, open the box and see what's still relevant. If none of the items are, donate them to charity. If the goals still haven't been achieved, either revise them or think up new, more realistic goals.

46. When taking down the Christmas lights, use sections of the current newspaper. Then next year, read what was happening in the world the previous year.

47. Research three people who share your birthday—one famous, one infamous, and one who is interestingly obscure. Example: January 16—supermodel Kate Moss, gangster Al Capone, and Robert Adler, the inventor of the TV remote control.

48. At least once a week, cut the toast into delightful bite-sized strips, sprinkle with cinnamon, and think of

mornings with Mom. And, remember, colorful people always indulge in real butter. Accept no substitutes.

49. Invent a whole new set of rules for the weekly golf/tennis/bowling match and convince your opponents to liven things up by playing by the wacky new rules.

50. When you're feeling flush, take some twenties or fifties and ask your spouse—and you have to be able to trust your spouse—to hide them throughout the house in book jackets, behind curtains and chairs, and in other out-of-the-way places, sort of like an Easter egg hunt. Then search for one every couple of weeks. Every time you find one, splurge on an elegant brunch that Sunday.

51. Enjoy doing your civic duty. Don't dodge jury duty—revel in it.

Colorful Days Diary

Hooray for me! After months of desperation, something I've been dreaming of and praying about finally happened on Tuesday. Yep, I got a job—important county work.

Jury duty!

Yesterday, a distinguished judge addressed me and about 120 fellow Westmoreland County citizens. He told us how we were there to provide the spiritual backbone to the best judicial system ever devised by mankind. Fortunes and lives would rise and fall on the collective wisdom we were about to bestow.

Pay would be nine dollars a day.

Most people would rather fake their own death before accepting jury duty. Not me. I couldn't wait. The night before, I did a little home barbering, picked out a nice shirt and coat, and took steps to ensure I wouldn't be too hungover to function for the important first day.

Of course, most people have jobs and obligations. They are engaged in productive lives. Me, I haven't worked in about five months. To be honest, I haven't done real work since I turned in my sauce-stained apron down at the old Pizza Hut.

I'm in a sort of transitional phase. I'm trying to move beyond writing magazine articles to becoming a full-fledged lah-de-dah author. I'm trying to get my satirical novel published. So instead of spending all my time getting paid to write magazine articles, I've been spending my time writing painstaking queries to agents who respond with terse, soul-scarring rejection letters.

Nine dollars a day would seem like a gaudy windfall.

Everyone jokes about jury duty, but it's a truly ennobling experience. It gives me the same sort of patriotic jolt I get when I walk into a voting booth. Or at least it used to be called a voting booth. These days it's more of an exposed sort of electronic voting station that always makes me suspicious that either my vote's not going to count or someone's going to sneak up behind me to bash me over the head for not voting what they think is the right way.

It was fun to watch the other prospective jurors walk in. There were so many friendly faces. I made snap judgments about all of them and uniformly came down with positive reactions. Seven hours of confined tedium later, some of those judgments would shift.

And the tedium began almost instantly. I was not among the group of fifty that was called to the courtroom for questioning. That was fine with me. I had my laptop and the *New York Times*, and I was eager to dive into Jere Longman's outstanding book, *Among the Heroes*, about the randomly assembled group of strangers who on September 11, 2001, deliberately crashed the hijacked United Flight 93 into a Shanksville field just forty minutes from my Western Pennsylvania home.

The choice of Longman's book was deliberate. The heroic story of Flight 93 restores my faith whenever I feel humanity is being disparaged. And in the jury room, we, too, were a random group of strangers perhaps capable of greatness. We weren't there to fight terrorists. Our battle was with boredom.

"You know, they should have a bowling alley in here to keep people from going crazy," one woman said.

A bearded man in bib overalls suggested a dartboard. A guy in a Cosby sweater lamented he didn't bring along some Trivial Pursuit cards.

It was starting to sound like a fine tavern for teetotalers.

I thought briefly about opening up my laptop and entertaining the folks by reading aloud some of my recent blog posts. But I'm not that kind of extrovert. And if I were, one day I'd eventually realize it and be forced to throw myself in front of a speeding bus.

I was really enjoying having nothing to do but read. It reminded of the great quote from Lord Babington Macaulay, "I would rather be a poor man in a garret with plenty of books than a king who did not love reading."

Of course, anytime you're immersed in that vast a sea of humanity, you're bound to run into a crappie or two, and I'm not talking about the freshwater sport fish.

This one wore a Steelers sweatshirt and kept a running commentary about the soap opera that played on the TV in the front of the big room. He followed each lewd comment with a nervous staccato laugh that sounded like someone had spilled a bucket of empty beer cans down a long flight of stairs.

The guy wouldn't shut up. Had he been on the ill-fated Flight 93, I wonder if the heroes would have turned on him before dealing with the terrorists. I would have argued that it should have been the priority.

Finally at 4:00 p.m. the jury commissioner came in, thanked us, and said we wouldn't be needed. We could all go home.

I was being fired!

I went up and pleaded with her to let me come back the next day.

"You're serious? You really want to come back?"

"Yes, I think this is something I could really be good at. I'm a good listener, and I didn't doze off once or try to kill that loud-mouthed jerk in the Steelers jersey."

"Your turn will come again, sir. We'll let you know."

"Will it be later this month? I'm sure I'll be available."

"It'll be in 2018."

Still, it had been a great day. I'd done my civic duty without incident. The government recognized my service and would pay me nine dollars.

Minus the six dollars it cost to park, that left me with a tidy three-dollar profit.

The urge to splurge was impossible to resist.

Tonight, I'm taking the girls out for gumballs!

52. On a night when you're supposed to bring home or cook dinner, use your cell phone's geographical anonymity to surprise your spouse. Call and say you're running late because the gang at work wanted to go out to have some drinks at a gentleman's club (or if you're a woman, someplace suitably scandalous). Make the call from one block away. Listen to your partner cursing and then apologize and hang up. Then run through the door carrying a bottle of wine and your spouse's favorite pizza.

53. Save all your found coins in a big jar—forever. You'll never save enough to make it worth spending, but it'll give you a tiny jolt of gentle joy each time you find a coin on the sidewalk.

54. Go to a fine Italian restaurant and order "turtle-lini." When the waiter acts confused, explain that you want stuffed shells, but you're bored with the name stuffed shells.

55. Go ahead. Stop in and see what the fortune-teller has to say.

56. Take a dart vacation. Put a map of the United States on the garage wall and decide where you're going by which state the dart hits. Every state in the land has beautiful tourist attractions. Let a kid throw the dart.

57. Pick a historical hero, someone you can admire without reservation. Learn all you can about that long-ago person. Then pick a living person, someone in your family or living in the neighborhood, and do the same.

58. Never let a political dispute hurt a friendship. Remember, politics is a pendulum. Those who are right today may be wrong tomorrow. And vice versa.

59. Invent a great, unique sandwich with all your favorite ingredients. Name it after yourself and serve it to friends. Then do the same with an enormous ice-cream sundae.

60. Celebrate the birthday of a favorite movie star with an in-home film festival of the star's hits. Suggestion: Jimmy Stewart, May 20, 1908; rent *Harvey*, *The Philadelphia Story*, and *The Man Who Shot Liberty Valance*. Make lots of popcorn.

61. No matter how fancy or refined the party you're hosting is, be sure to string up rows and rows of delightful novelty lights—hot peppers, snowmen, tropical fish.

62. Create a Hall of Fame shelf for yourself where you put reminders of your life's little victories. Then create a penalty box in the garage where you put golf clubs, tools, or other underperforming everyday items.

63. Get a bird feeder and put it in sight of your kitchen window. Then buy a bird-watching book.

64. Put away the fashionably popular albums and instead support and enjoy some obscure artist without an enormous national following. Then drop the artist's name at the next party in a group of people and you'll find at least one instant friend. Suggested artists: Lucinda Williams, Delbert McClinton, Todd Snider.

Colorful Days Diary

One of the great things about being invited to be an adjunct professor at a local university, as I've been, is that it instantly invests you with an undeserved aura of authority.

Point Park University in Pittsburgh has for three years done this with me. They've asked me to teach creative nonfiction to their journalism graduate students. In this role, I'm expected to prepare them for the future of earning a living submitting stories for print. Clearly, the students don't listen to the thrust of my talk or else they'd be, as I often advise, dashing out the door to sign up for pre-law.

But it's the weekly opportunity for crackpot declarations and petty despotism that gives me the most pleasure.

For instance, earlier this spring, the local paper ran a story about a world-renowned record collector and illustrated it with a picture of him holding a rare copy of the 1971 Rolling Stones album, *Sticky Fingers*. The cutline said the record was worth $10,000.

I brandished the paper before the class, read the cutline, and asked, "Can anyone here point out the libelous inaccuracy that got past the reporter, the editor, and a squad of foul coffee-breathed copy editors?"

As usual, eight students looked like they were about to fall asleep on their doodles, eight stared zombie-like out the window, and the menacing twosome in the back row looked like they were intensifying their plot to kill me.

When no one spoke, I dramatically leaned forward on the lectern, pounded it with my fist, and said, "Every single Rolling Stones album ever made is worth $10,000!"

I then launched into a lengthy pontification about The Stones and their importance and even squeezed in some of my favorite Stones trivia such as: The Stones are the only band ever to include listening instructions on an album. It's true. On the seminal rock classic *Let It Bleed*, in big block letters at the bottom are the words, "THIS RECORD SHOULD BE PLAYED LOUD."

Amen.

I'm one of those obnoxious music snobs who's convinced himself that no one has better or more refined taste in music than I do. My iTunes library has 7,627 items I could play nonstop for 21.4 days.

When I began converting my massive CD collection to iTunes about three years ago, I weeded out all the crap. Now, I rigorously check my play counts to make sure nothing's falling through the cracks. In two years, I've played every one of the songs—not counting the occasional Christmas ditty—at least four times.

(The top three most played as of July 11, 2009, are the following: Ray Davies, "After the Fall," ninety-four times; Bob Dylan, "Workingman's Blues #2," ninety-two times; Van Morrison, "Celtic New Year," ninety-one times—and I defy anyone to listen to any of these gems once and not feel compelled to repeat them until the batteries fizzle.)

But because I never listen to CDs anymore and, unlike old LPs, have no sentimental attachments to the tiny shinies, it was time to haul the bunch of them to the local flea market and set up shop.

My wife came along for base mercenary reasons. I was there to make sure the music got in the hands of people who needed it most. Business was brisk.

A kid of about sixteen came up and asked if I had any Doors.

"The Doors," I scolded, "are the most overrated band in the history of music. Here's the most underrated one." I handed him a stack of CDs by The Kinks.

A middle-aged man in a Hawaiian shirt approached and asked if I had any Jimmy Buffett.

"I did about twenty years ago when he was still relevant," I said. "If you like Buffett, take this Todd Snider CD, *Songs for the Daily Planet*. He's better and you won't risk looking like some silly part-time pirate once a year."

My wife and I had a great chat with two guys who looked like they were two hours overdue for their first Sunday beers (it was 10:30 a.m.). They bought some James McMurtry, some Drive-By Truckers, and showed impeccable taste by snapping up Steve Earle's *Transcendental Blues*. I was so overjoyed at meeting kindred spirits I handed them Robert Earl Keen's *Gringo Honeymoon* and *Letters to Laredo* by the peerless Joe Ely.

I know I'll someday run into these guys again in either a roadside honky-tonk or, perhaps, a Lubbock, Texas, drunk tank, and we'll have a great time till our wives show up with bail bucks.

I do so little in this life to help my fellow man that I felt a true surge of humanity whenever I could give someone something like Van Morrison's *The Healing Game* or *Shangri-La* by Mark Knopfler.

I know that mousy young girl's life is going to change because I was the one who told her to go home and listen to *Car Wheels on a Gravel Road* by Lucinda Williams, and that maybe that kid who walked away with *If Heartbreaks Were Highways* by Los Gravediggers will ditch his crabby girlfriend and his dead-end job and strike out to hit it rich in Vegas.

All told, we made $329. Sure I had hopes it would be more, but reality checked in when a guy offered me a buck for *Let It Bleed* by The Rolling Stones.

I said, "Mister, that and every other Rolling Stones CD is worth $10,000."

He looked at me like I was a lunatic and said, "I'll give you two dollars."

Sold!

I'm pretty sure I could have persuaded him to pay my price, but it was looking like it might rain.

And, honestly, it didn't matter much to me. Gandhi died broke, too.

65. Find out what your phone number spells. That way, instead of using the cumbersome, "Call me at 614-233-4483," which no one will remember, just say, "Call me at 614 BEE-HIVE," which everyone will remember.

66. Be as comfortable in dive bars as you are in elegant restaurants. Learn to speak the language of both crooks and kings.

67. Next time you find reason to go to the local public library, sneak over into the children's section and read an old Dr. Seuss book you remember enjoying as a child.

If you don't have a reason to go to the public library, make one up. Wonderful things happen there.

68. Write down this Robert Louis Stevenson quote and put it somewhere you'll see it each and every day: "There is no duty we so much underrate as the duty of being happy."

69. When you're done with the drudgery of paying the monthly bills, get in the habit of unwinding by calling an old friend with whom you haven't spoken in more than a year. Just to chat and reminisce about the good times you've shared.

70. Colorful people point out whenever it is apropos that good mimes can be safe, but never sound.

71. If you live in a small, urban apartment, cultivate a small coffee-can garden on your porch. Do the same if you live on a big farm.

72. Spend a warm spring afternoon planting tree saplings scattered along vacant land you pass every day on your way to work. Enjoy monitoring their growth during traffic jams.

73. Live your life like you're a devoted stationary salesman, always pushing the envelope.

74. Every ten years, whether you need one or not, visit the local pound and get a new dog or cat. Every time you see the dog's wagging tail or hear the cat purr, you'll feel a little jolt of joyful pride for your role in saving the tiny beast's life.

75. If you haven't ever done it, make it a point to attend a Major League Baseball game and sit someplace where you have a better than average chance of snagging a foul ball. Catching one is one of life's great wee pleasures.

76. Learn to accompany each sneeze with a nonsense phrase or word—"Gizzleploop!"

77. Once a year, spend a morning preparing mountains of fried peanut butter and banana sandwiches while listening to great iconic rock by the man known as the King. Then, go ahead, strap on a bib and eat like Elvis.

78. Be unconventional, even when it's inconvenient or leads to ridicule. Unconventional is its own kind of cool.

Colorful Days Diary

The boys in the bar were making fun of how long my hair was getting. Understand, when I'm talking about the boys in the bar, I don't mean Vidal Sassoon, Paul Mitchell, or Jay Sebring.

These guys don't cut hair. Heck, these guys barely have hair. My bar, The Pond, is not some swanky Manhattan cocktail lounge populated by thin pretty boys and girls fresh from their fashion shoots. It's what me and my underage friends used to deride as an "old man's bar" before we all became old men.

It's a friendly tavern, but on some days there is a throwback element to a 1950s sort of danger, like the kind George Bailey finds in Nick's after his "wish I'd never been born" prayer turns Bedford Falls into Pottersville.

In fact, one bartender is exactly like Nick, the owner of the place where Bailey and apprentice angel Clarence Oddbody retire for a double whiskey and a "mulled wine, heavy on the cinnamon and light on the cloves," respectively.

The exotic order prompts Nick to seethe, "Look, mister—we serve hard drinks in here for men who want to get drunk fast, and we don't need any characters around to give the joint 'atmosphere.' Is that clear, or do I have to slip you my left for a convincer?"

That's what it's like on Tuesdays when Angry Bill's working, only with Bill, every other word would have NBC censors diving on the five-second delay the way heroes dive on live grenades.

I'm often the target for ridicule because I consider it my duty to give the joint atmosphere. I differ from most of my fellow drinkers in that I dress dapper, profess liberal opinions, and use common silverware for things like salad and spaghetti.

If they ever start stocking mulled wine, why, I'll be the first to order a big snifter full and load it up with the cinnamon I keep with the cloves and other spices I always carry around in my handy little fanny pack.

My critics are strictly the ball cap and tube sock crowd. And that's not even the most noticeable difference in our appearance.

That would be hair. I have it. They do not.

In fact, I have a lot of it. It's thinning a bit, but what I have behaves like the East Germans did after the Berlin Wall came crashing down. It's having a party.

I go as long as eight weeks without getting it cut. I do this for many reasons. It saves money. It saves time. It keeps me from having to go to that awful unisex salon where I feel they're psychologically severing things more dear to me than hair every time I enter and am assaulted by music from people like Beyoncé.

The days when men with long, lively hair were considered effeminate ended throughout most of America about thirty years ago. That means it'll be another fifteen years or so before it ends here in Western Pennsylvania.

But I argue that these men so concerned about their masculinity are actually behaving more ladylike than I.

They devote more time and product to their appearances than I ever do. I get out of the shower, run a brush through the noodles, and I'm done. The whole procedure takes maybe twelve seconds. Then the hair is at liberty to do as it pleases for twenty-four hours.

If tedious facial shaving is any indicator, my tormentors probably spend fifteen or twenty minutes every other day gazing into the mirror at their apelike faces as they try not to nick their noggins with the buzzing little groomers.

The smooth result is that when two of them put their heads together to talk confidentially about guns, Sarah Palin, or NASCAR, the combined effect looks like one wide bottom is trying to make an angry point by mooning some invisible cross-bar antagonist.

Of course, like most bar arguments, this one is an utterly pointless diversion. Increasing numbers of my once stout hairs are becoming cowardly deserters. They go AWOL, and one day I recognize that I, too, will be just another butt head sitting around the old man's bar.

Oh, well. That's the circle of life.

Hair today. Gone tomorrow.

79. Find a place in your living room for a small aquarium. Spend relaxing time staring at it instead of the TV.

80. If you're tempted to get a provocative bumper sticker, don't just get one. Get about a dozen. That way people won't confuse you with a boring single-issue motorist.

81. Take a deep breath. Now take another. Studies show that slow, deep breathing is probably the best anti-stress medicine we have. And the less your brain is occupied dealing with stress, the more time it'll have for creative thinking.

82. Become a devotee of one super group—The Beatles or The Rolling Stones. It'll ensure you'll be able to find some common ground with anyone with whom you get stuck in an elevator.

83. Learn the details and importance of a nearby Civil War battlefield or other site of historical significance.

84. For parties, always keep at least one novelty bar of soap in the house. And, really, shouldn't all soap come in funny shapes?

85. Before the baby is born, designate one door jamb or basement pillar to gauge the growth spurts of the growing child. Don't forget to include the dates.

86. Collect a handful of sand from the beach or dirt from each national park where you vacation and put it in its own little spice jar. Label the jar with the name of the place and put the happy memories on a shelf. Add a sign saying something like "The Spices of Life."

87. Suggest to friends that one day all violent crime will cease when innovative ammunition companies develop "smart" bullets that will decide after exiting the gun whether the target deserves lethal ventilation. Predict that some bullets will actually reverse and strike the gunman.

88. Colorful people take at least one hot-air balloon ride in their lives.

89. Volunteer for everything. Whether it's a clown seeking participants for a slapstick circus act or a US Army colonel asking for someone brave to take a death-defying mission, be a volunteer.

90. Wear unusual underwear. Always. Most days, no one will ever find out, but you just never know.

91. Spend a weekend willing yourself to blink more slowly. That way you'll be able to savor all the joyful things everyone says go by in the blink of an eye.

92. Read the words to "The Star-Spangled Banner." Then every time it's played at a sporting event, point out to people nearby that our national anthem ends in a question mark. And, c'mon, sing it loud and sing it proud!

93. Mow the lawn in different patterns each week. Ask the neighbors to vote on their favorite.

94. Never ignore even the smallest courtesy. If someone holds a door for you, look them in the eye and say an enthusiastic, "Thank you!" Let the kind person feel like they've just done you the world's biggest favor. Maybe they'll be tempted to do you another one.

95. If you see them on some desolate highway, they're hitchhikers and could be dangerous. But if you see them standing at your local bus stop in the pouring rain, they're just soggy neighbors. Go ahead—stop the car and give them a ride.

96. Read the classics—Steinbeck, Twain, Hemingway—you skimmed over or ignored in high school English. Not only will you find them immensely fulfilling, but you'll be given fresh insight as to why teenagers aren't nearly as smart as they think they are (or you thought you were).

97. Celebrate March 7 by reminding everyone you call that it was on that day in 1876 that Alexander Graham Bell was issued a patent for the first telephone. Ask callers to imagine how the first phones would have sounded if Bell's name had been Alexander Graham Horn.

98. Get the *Roadfood* book by Jane and Michael Stern (Broadway Books). It's the self-billed "coast-to-coast guide to 600 of the best barbecue joints, lobster shacks, ice cream parlors, highway diners and much, much more." Keep it in your car and you'll be surprised how many times you drive fifty miles out of your way for a great authentic meal. Colorful people make it a point to always avoid fast foods.

99. Get a living will and update your mortal will. In both documents, include instructions that will provoke joyful bursts of inappropriate laughter at your funeral. The leavening aspects of humor will never be more welcome, and your loved ones will be grateful.

100. It bears repeating. The five key ingredients to letting love grow are these: play, tickle, cuddle, kiss, hug. Apply generously, especially to the wee ones.

101. Ask dog owners if theirs is a watchdog. If they say yes, ask if it was hard to teach it to tell time and if it was a clockdog before it graduated into becoming a watchdog.

102. Once a year, rent a movie that's funny and full of the kind of ear-blistering language you were forbidden from using as a child. Anyone raised properly doesn't use that kind of language in polite society. Much. That's what makes it so darn funny. Suggestions: *Midnight Run*, starring Robert De Niro, and *Slapshot*, starring Paul Newman.

Colorful Days Diary

It came to my attention this spring that a certain number of impressionables were occasionally checking in on my blog, and that meant I regretfully had to renege on a previous promise.

When I was sketching out the likely future of these writings, I'd broadly hinted that they would contain lots and lots of profanity. There'd be, I'd said, ribald references, double and triple entendres, and the kind of straight blue profanity you hear in foxholes and on construction sites.

Not now.

I don't want to risk corrupting any of the youth with language they've been warned repeatedly against using by austere authority figures at home, at school, and in their churches. Corrupting morals in the cyber way is such a tawdry business.

Especially as long as I still reserve the right to enjoy doing so in person. One of the great thrills of corrupting innocents is seeing an alarmed and electric look steal across their faces when they realize that always being good isn't always the only option. And one of the easiest ways to do this is to drop an unexpected f-bomb in an inappropriate place like, say, a classroom of higher education.

When teaching undergrad and grad journalism students at Point Park University in Pittsburgh, one of the first things I always do—right after urgently advising the students against having anything to do with journalism—is to announce that the class will include profanity.

I do this because you can see the jolts of increased enthusiasm ripple through their postures. I may only do so two or three times the entire semester, but the announcement gives me a license to swear, sort of making me agent "Double Oh S---!"

I don't know what it is about forbidden words that makes them so deliciously enticing, but that's simply the case with so-called swear words and any of the other fruits we forbid. Just try watching the sanitized version of *The Sopranos* on A&E.

I cringe for the franchise whenever I see an enraged Paulie Walnuts about to ventilate some hapless bookie and having the puritanical censors dub in place of a stream of vicious profanity, "You bad stupid man!" before he commits a more ballistic sort of obscenity on the person.

My wife and I are enormous fans of *Seinfeld*-creator Larry David's *Curb Your Enthusiasm*. It's loaded with wonderful, over-the-top profanity that always keeps us cackling.

Alas, it's a topic with which our eight-year-old daughter, the product of two profanity-spewing parents, is beginning to struggle. She's forever narcing on one or the other of us for saying words she's apparently heard forbidden in the second grade.

For me, it's been fun watching her learn about rudimentary profanity from her mother in traffic, her mother at card-gobbling ATMs, her mother running late, and her mother whenever her father's too hungover to do simple household chores like brush his teeth.

Two years ago, our daughter enlivened the Thanksgiving Day table by matter-of-factly announcing, "The f-word rhymes with Chuck." My white-haired mother's reaction was as compelling as anything ever produced for *The Waltons*.

But I didn't flinch. I've told her many times that there are no bad words. There are only bad times to say some words like, for instance, right after the Thanksgiving meal blessing. Still, it dismays me to see that our societal revulsion for some of these great, colorful words is so formidable that she is being coerced into thinking some words are too powerful, too awful to ever be uttered.

To that I ask the universal question (but will paraphrase in keeping with my pledge to sanitize this forum), what the heck?

A perfectly timed blast of profanity is always a welcome addition to any otherwise stoic conversation. It frees up the minds. It expands the boundaries and bestows a sort of democratic camaraderie that brings noblemen and peasants to the same level.

For my part, I will continue to shout profanities from the rooftops, in the classrooms, on the golf courses, from atop my bar stool, and anyplace where a single well-timed profanity might jar free men and women everywhere into realizing that we all lose when language is shackled to a caste system of good or evil.

Because the judicious use of profanity doesn't denigrate man, it ennobles him.

I swear.

103. Let the calendar dictate your ethnic meals. Enjoy a Mexican restaurant on Cinco de Mayo (May 5). Go to Chinatown to celebrate the Chinese New Year (varies each winter). Make reservations at a great French restaurant on Bastille Day (July 14). And be sure to enjoy at least one hot dog each and every Fourth of July.

104. Next time you're out of town, purchase and mail two postcards—one scenic, one sexy—and mail them to a friend at the same time. Chances are the scenic one will zip right through while the sexy one will be held up due

to unusual delays, especially if they are mailed to snowy destinations in the dead of winter.

105. Ask your friends how their parents are doing. Genuinely care about their answer. It's something that ought to matter to everyone.

106. Ruthlessly haggle over prices at yard sales. If it's for sale for fifty dollars, offer ten. If it's going for a quarter, tell them you'll pay a nickel. Don't do it to be cheap. Do it for the thrill of the bargain.

107. Colorful conversation starter: next time you hear someone say, "Nature abhors a vacuum," ask if that explains why the world is so dirt-y.

108. Be a good listener, always … Did you catch that? Be a good listener, always.

109. Develop a conversational understanding of all the world's major religions, and an anecdotal familiarity with at least one of the really wacky ones.

110. Keep scores, but never settle them. Keeping score can lead to satisfying moments when you recall those who said you couldn't do something. Settling scores can lead to jail sentences.

111. Turn Saturday wake-ups into musical mornings. Have everyone in the family sing their every word. *"It's time for me to take a shower! Please, please, please have the coffee and the paper ready for me!"*

112. Volunteer to work at the local ice-cream stand for free one night or afternoon a week each summer in exchange for free ice cream. By the end of the first shift, you'll find

the work so pleasantly satisfying you'll be offering to pay them for the privilege of working a second shift.

113.   Buy an episode guide to one of your favorite shows and develop an encyclopedic knowledge of something joyfully meaningless like *Green Acres*.

Colorful Days Diary

It was the greatest letter I'd ever received, and it was nearly lost forever because, with the exception of one shining superstar, my home is in Hooterville.

It was a personal letter from one of the most famous people on the planet. It said he looked forward to reading what I wrote every day, and he just wanted to let me know how much he enjoyed my work.

It was sent December 23, 2008, and it finally landed in my hands on March 26, 2009. It took ninety-three days to travel two miles.

Don't blame the US Post Office. Blame Hooterville.

Hooterville was the fictional site of the still uproarious TV Land staple, *Green Acres*. It was a town populated by dimwits who were forever causing vein-popping consternation for erstwhile attorney Oliver Wendell Douglas, the naive farmer who ditched lawyering in New York for the bucolic life among the country rubes.

It's one of my favorite shows, and one of my favorite episodes dealt with the fury that Douglas, played by the inestimable Eddie Albert, felt on Old Mail Day down at Sam Drucker's general store.

Old Mail Day was the festival when Hootervillians gathered to get the old mail that Sam had misplaced or found when he was cleaning behind the pickle barrel. Many once-important pieces of mail were distributed. I remember Fred Ziffel was stunned to read he'd been drafted to serve—in World War I.

I thought about that episode when my good friend Dave said he had a letter for me. Dave owns the ground-floor tavern and rents one of the three second-floor apartments above his business to me for cheap. It's where I keep a shabby little office and am always handy if the bar runs short of thirsty customers.

He asked if I was missing any mail. I said, "I don't receive any mail here. All my mail goes to my home address."

"Well, you got one letter here that was dated December 23. Your idiot neighbor upstairs got it by mistake and never bothered to give it over."

His harsh assessment of my neighbor, John, was correct. He's an absolute idiot. He'd fit right in on *Green Acres*. Arnold Ziffel could wear an "I'm with Stupid" shirt around John and no one would dispute the pig.

Still, John and I are on good terms. If I restricted my friendships and conversations to only intelligent people, it would be a very lonely existence and I'd have to stop even talking to myself. It was strange he hadn't just given it to me.

"He said he felt bad. He found it under a stack of old papers he was about to throw away. It's a letter from Arnold Palmer."

Well, you could have knocked me off my bar stool with a feather—and I was just sipping my first beer, so don't factor inebriation into the equation. I was stunned.

I looked up across the bar and there on the television was Arnold Palmer himself. By the most surreal of coincidences, a ninety-three-day-old letter from Palmer was delivered to me while we were watching Arnold Palmer being interviewed on television about the Arnold Palmer Invitational golf tournament being played at Bay Hill Club & Lodge in Orlando.

For ten years, I've been doing the "Amazing but True Golf Facts" one-page-per-day calendars. Every Christmas, I'd always take a few up to Palmer's longtime assistant, the great Doc Giffin. I never dared try to talk to Palmer himself, even though Doc told me the boss was an enthusiastic reader of my little pages.

I was doing a lot of golf writing in 2005 when Doc asked me to do a major website project working with Palmer web wizard Scott Curry. It was my job to go through five decades of old newspaper clips detailing every newsworthy activity in which Palmer was engaged on every day of his life. That meant going through more than 20 legal boxes that contained newspaper clippings of every time Palmer's name was mentioned in a newspaper or magazine dating back to the 1950s.

Then it was Scott's job to corral what may be the world's most unique celebrity biography and bestow it with flair befitting a legend. It's cool. Check out the timeline at www.arnoldpalmer.com.

And it is a momentous life of rarely equaled exuberance. Set aside the ninety-three professional golfing victories, the legions of adoring fans, and all the indelible and enduring charity work, and it's one of the most amazing lives in American history.

An expert pilot, he's set around-the-world aviation records, is best buddies with several presidents, and golfed with all but two of them since Ike. Bill Clinton says one of the great perks of the office is getting to play golf with Arnold Palmer. Kirk Douglas said in 1970 that no one—not Sinatra, John Wayne, or Ronald Reagan—has more charisma than Palmer.

Even though I began interviewing him on a regular basis, I was still convinced that the first time he was ever going to utter my name was when he'd say, "We have to fire this Chris Rodell!"

Now here I was holding a letter from the man himself. I opened it and read it aloud to my friends at the bar.

Dear Chris,

Many thanks for the new 2009 calendar. You do know how much I enjoy reading the amazing golf facts each day. Even when the day is done, I tear off the page and keep it for future reference. My very best holiday wishes to you and your family for a Happy Holiday.

Sincerely,
Arnold

I'm starting to think one of the most famous men in the world considers me a friend. And now I have evidence that I'm not a Hooterville kind of crazy.

Sometimes some of the best things in life are hiding just out of reach behind life's proverbial pickle barrel.

I hope there's some good news out there that you don't know about that one day, maybe months from now, will make your day the way that letter made mine.

And best wishes to you and your family for a very Merry March Christmas.

114. Every April 1st for as many years as it takes for them to catch on, place a call to the same person and leave a message from "Mr. Bear," "Mr. Lyon," or "Mr. John Deere," and then leave the number for the local zoo. Always call the zoo later that day and say, "Hi, this is Mr. Bear. Have there been any calls for me?" The next year, leave a message from a Mr. L. E. Funt.

115. Inflate your high school SAT scores to preposterous levels. Tell people you scored 1775. When they point out it's impossible to score more than 1600, make up a brilliant lie to justify the impossibility.

116. Understand your life will be appreciably more balanced and sane if you wake up every Monday and realize your job isn't nearly as important as you think it is.

117. Emphasize to friends that the snack would still taste and look the same, but they would take on a whole new connotation if they were spelled "FreeToes."

118. The difference between right and wrong is confusing to young children. Instead, teach them light and dark. Use your own examples for dark, but for light use The Muppets.

119. Colorful conversation starter: tell people that it's easy to understand that our predecessors from five hundred years ago thought the earth was flat and that scientific advances led them to conclude the world was round. Ask people if they thought that in between those conventional wisdoms someone might have proposed the globe was cubic.

120. If you haven't been in more than ten years, pack up the kids and head to Niagara Falls. Sure you've seen it in pictures and maybe memories, but seeing it again will leave you speechless save for one word: wow.

121. Rent the 1993 movie *Searching for Bobby Fischer*, a movie about chess that will leave you with the same exhilarating feeling you got the first time you saw *Rocky*. Then get a cheap chess set and get good at the game.

122. Extravagantly overtip friendly, underpaid waitresses who often spend long days and nights away from small children to bring you a hot meal. At night when they go home and are soaking their aching feet, they say prayers asking God to bless people like you.

123. When doing dreary everyday housework—dishes, changing diapers—keep a stopwatch handy and treat the chore like a NASCAR pit stop. Challenge your housemates to beat your time.

124. Your marriage will suffer a reduction in the number and duration of rough patches it experiences if you understand from day one that true love is not an emotion. True love is a decision.

125. Gauge the age of people you meet by asking them if they know who'd answer the phone if you dialed the number 867-5309. With everyone's number being concealed under a name, Jenny's is the last number humanity will ever collectively remember.

126. Never let a grudge fester. Too many people bury the hatchet and immediately try and remember where they left the shovel.

127. Don't be a snob. Read the tabloids. They are guaranteed great fun and show elegant celebrities with fingers up their noses.

128. Think about it: in your lifetime, you or someone you know will vacation on the surface of the moon. Mention it to friends when they ask your advice on a vacation destination. Speculate on the heavenly possibilities.

129. Next time someone confuses you with a long-lost friend, play along. If they think you're Bill, become Bill and give them a good story to tell back home.

Colorful Days Diary

I had my stand-offish Sunday morning face on. I hadn't showered and didn't want any human interaction other than those six or so words I'd exchange with the clerk where I buy gas.

I finished pumping, crossed the parking lot, and pulled open the door to the local Sheetz convenience mart.

It was like I walked into a one-man surprise party and was the guest of honor.

"Bill! Hey, Bill! Man, is it good to see you!"

I looked around. I was all alone. I was Bill.

Now, careful readers of my work know that I am not Bill and have never pretended to be Bill.

But the elderly stranger who thought I was Bill was thrilled to see someone he was convinced was Bill.

He was probably in his late sixties. He had a very kind face that was enlivened by seeing what he thought was an old friend. He had his fist salute extended and was waiting for me to bump knuckles.

I realized I was in a common social predicament. He'd confused me with a good friend.

He looked coherent, but who knows? Maybe he was one of our numerous village idiots. I'm friends with most of them, but they are accumulating like snow these days, and it's difficult to keep track of them all.

What was I to do?

I raised my fist, gave him my warmest buddy-buddy greeting, and said, "Hey, how the hell you been! You look great!"

And he did. He looked like I look when I'm driving down the road and hear John Fogerty and Creedence singing, *"Doo! Doo! Doo! Lookin' out my back door!"*

He was delighted.

My still-slumbering mind was racing through dozens of calculations. What was the risk here? Should I let him down gently or play along? What if the real Bill walked in?

You can converse with a stranger for about ninety seconds of generic conversation involving some form of the question, how are you?

Then the gentleman upped the ante. He wanted to know how Bonnie was doing.

We'd reached a turning point. I was left with a choice of either backing down and, perhaps, ruining the splendid start to his day, or pushing another stack of lies to the center of the table.

"She's great! Just finished all her Christmas shopping. Her mom slipped on the snow last week, but she'll be all right."

He was sorry to hear that. He asked me how work was going, allowing me the opportunity to venture into a rare burst of honesty.

"It's been slow, but things are turning around. I'm optimistic better days are on the way."

The guy at the counter was buying lottery tickets, and the other clerk was fetching change. My high-wire act couldn't endure forever. *C'mon, let's get those registers ringing.*

"And how about Mark? How's he doing?"

He was a family guy, so I figured Mark was my son. I know kids today have their problems, but it was the holidays. I wasn't going to ruin his day by telling him Mark's in rehab.

"He's great. He's up at Clarion University. He wants to be a veterinarian."

This pleased him. He had fond memories of Mark.

The guy at the counter was putting his change in his wallet, and I was hoping Bonnie and I didn't have any more kids.

Finally, it was his turn to pay just as the other clerk stepped up. At just about the same time, we both realized our little holiday was over. We looked each other in the eye and put our right arm around the other's left shoulder for brief man hugs.

It was a beautiful moment.

We wished each other a Merry Christmas, and I told him I'd be sure to tell Bonnie he'd said hello.

It reminded me of the final scene of the great 1995 movie, *Smoke*, in which the Harvey Keitel character tells the William Hurt character about an encounter he had with an elderly blind woman who thought he was her nephew. He wound up staying for dinner. Hurt thinks he made it all up, but as the credits role, they show the scene he recalled, as the Tom Waits song "Innocent When You Dream" plays.

It's magnificent.

I thought about the right and wrong of what I'd done as I drove home. I'd told a slew of lies to a kindhearted gentleman who may one day wind up very confused next time he sees Bill or Bonnie out getting gas.

But I think my bigger sin was not the lies. It was the size of them.

They were all too small.

I should have told him our bowling team won the league championship, Bonnie had a book of poems published, her mom had won the state lottery, and Mark was studying to be an astronaut.

I should have told him they'd discovered a cure for cancer, the wars were all over, and they'd discovered a way to fax leftovers to the hungry.

I should have told him that this Christmas everything was going to be all right.

Because, really, that's what he wanted Bill to tell him. It's what we all want to hear.

I hope even a fraction of all that happens.

And I hope Bill, Bonnie, and Mark have a wonderful Christmas and Mark doesn't ruin the holiday by drinking too much.

130. Develop the same confidential sort of relationship with the owner of a small bookstore that you do with a trusted physician. A good doctor will keep your body fit. A familiar book store owner can do the same for your imagination and intellect.

131. Enjoy a Chinese dinner with someone special. Spend a quiet part of the meal composing personal fortune cookie notes for each other to be shared after the feast.

132. Get the entire catalog of the 1990's band, The Traveling Wilburys. It's just two albums, but the twenty-one outstanding songs composed by Bob Dylan, Tom Petty, Jeff Lynne, George Harrison, and Roy Orbison are quickly becoming forgotten by all but the most colorful people.

133. Become a squirrel trainer. Learn to sit quietly in a squirrel-filled park with a big bag of peanuts. Eventually, the nervous critters will overcome their jitters and snatch the nut right from your fingers. It may take all summer, and it may only happen once, but the delight will be worth it.

134. Send the batch of Christmas cards you didn't get to during the holidays in early February. Tell the recipients that you were so eager to wish them a Merry Christmas, you just couldn't wait until next December.

135. Understand that porn directors are the only people who should be allowed to say, "Man up!"

136. On the hottest, most skin-blistering day in August, drive to a cool mountain stream. If it takes you longer than an hour, pack a lunch and a six-pack. Dangle the six-pack and your bare feet in the water while you're reading a book about the arctic perils of climbing Mt. Everest.

137. Treat everyone, be they bums or beauty queens, exactly the same. If you're going to be a jerk to one class of people, you'll be more respected if you're a jerk to all the others. But, please, don't be a jerk. To anyone.

138. Be sure to laugh out loud. A lot.

139. Never read a book without having at least a slim dictionary within arm's length. Look up every word you don't absolutely understand. Then write the word down and use it until you're confident of its meaning and application. A muscular vocabulary can get you out of more trouble and into more cool situations than a muscular body ever will.

140. Everyone knows to visit the Statue of Liberty when visiting New York City. Whenever you visit someplace new, always call the local Convention & Visitors Bureau and ask about a city's hidden treasures. Ask for discounts and freebies, too. If they have 'em, you'll get 'em.

141. Become a twenty-dollar millionaire. You'll be amazed at what great, fawning service you get at airports, restaurants, and hotels just by dropping an Andy Jackson in someone's palm. The word gets around quick, and you'll jump to the front of any line like the Invisible Man.

142. The calendar year is getting old when the leaves begin to fall, but that doesn't mean you have to. Every year, rake the leaves into a big pile in the backyard and dive in like an Olympic gold medalist. The soul-refreshing fun will stiffen your spine for any bitter winter.

143. Become a silly sort of Deep Throat for a local paper or TV station. If you remember your history, Deep Throat was the murky source that helped Woodward & Bernstein

topple the Nixon presidency during the Watergate scandal. That's historic, but no fun. Choose a stylish reporter and send them interesting feature story ideas from your neighborhood. Who knows? Maybe you'll one day qualify for a profile.

144. One of the most effective TV ads of all time ran in Alabama and starred the late Crimson Tide coach Paul "Bear" Bryant on behalf of the local phone company. In his stern voice, Bryant said directly to the camera, "Call your mama," as scripted. Then he ad-libbed, "I wish I could." Do you need it any clearer? Call your mama!

145. Chop or gather your own firewood. If you don't have a fireplace, do it for an elderly neighbor or just for the splendid exercise, and just because firewood is one of the few things in life that really does grow on trees.

Colorful Days Diary

I was thrilled, as I always am, when a stranger e-mailed me this morning asking about how he could get some free firewood.

As anyone who's ever seen the home page of www.chrisrodell. com knows, I'm the world's leading purveyor of free firewood. No joke. I'll send anyone, anywhere in North America, free firewood.

With home fuel and heating prices skyrocketing, can anyone name a better deal?

Of course, you can't.

It all started about fifteen years ago. My wife and I had a lovely little house with a cozy fireplace. I pity those of you who live in places like Arizona or Florida, which suffer from year-round sunshine. You'll never know the pleasure of cuddling up with a loved one in front of a warming fire, charming fireplace implements at your side, while the wind's blowing blizzards and trash cans across the desolate lawn.

Go ahead, feel free to pity me right back this February when cabin fever has us all so crazy we're ready to use those charming fireplace implements to bash each other's brains in.

But to enjoy the fire, you need the one essential ingredient—and I'm not talking about a robust bulls-eye spark.

You need wood. Lots of it. And for that, you need an authentic woodsman.

I'd been warned that most woodsmen, around here at least, are among the most boring carbon-based life forms on the planet. I was told they spend long days out there among the oaks, maples, and pines, and that they must spend most of that lonely time trying to converse with the bark.

This I found to be true. The woodsmen I'd hired to bring me a cord or two each fall universally seemed—and pardon the pun—*stumped* whenever I'd speak back.

Plus, they seemed to be a bit—and here I go again—*shady* in their woodsmen ethics. They'd bring less than promised or bring lettuce-green wood that just insolently hissed at me rather than combust.

That I didn't mind. What I could not tolerate was that not a one of them ever got my firewood joke. And, dang it, it's funny. I'd spring it on them each time when we'd finished stacking.

I'd say, "Well, friend, how much do I owe you for this 'ere wood?"

"I reckon (many woodsmen are reckoners) you owe me $125."

At this point, no matter what the price, I'd feign shock. "Gee, $125! That's a lot of money. I guess firewood doesn't grow on trees!"

Silence. Nothing.

See, it's funny because firewood is one of the few products you can buy that actually *does* grow on trees.

Had I ever found one bearded woodsman who slapped his torn jeans and said, "Ha! That's a good one! Firewood don't grow on trees! Ha! Ha!" I would have invited him inside for a beer and signed a twenty-five-year contract for annual delivery.

But the reaction was always the same: dumbfounded silence.

So I decided to heck with the whole sorry bunch of them and ran out and bought my own chainsaw. Each year now, I head into the woods and harvest my own timber, something that marginally makes me, a guy who talks and types for a living, feel at least a little bit like a manly dude.

And each year as I kneel down and light the first warming fire of the fall, my wife expresses her gratitude and support by saying something like, "I'm amazed you've made it another year without chopping off one of your limbs or being crushed to death by a falling tree."

So if you've never done so, please take a minute to visit www. chrisrodell.com and be sure to let me know if you need any free firewood.

And to my new friend, Dave S. in Glenview, Illinois, you can expect your shipment to arrive in the next week. Look for it in your mailbox.

It'll be free. It'll be wood. And it'll burn. If properly lit under mild wind conditions, there ought to be enough to set the delivery envelope ablaze. I suggest you put some paper and twigs around it if you want to kindle a bigger fire.

But first you'd better find an honest local woodsman. And good luck with that.

Those guys don't exactly grow on trees either.

146. A popular mid-Atlantic chain of convenience marts is named Sheetz after the owning family. If you're ever in one, compliment the clerk on the vast array of goods. Then ask where they keep the sheets. They don't sell sheets, you'll be told. Ask them then why they confuse the public by naming the place after one of the few items they do not sell.

147. Write fan letters to obscure actors or musicians. Chances are they'll write back and will fondly remember your goodhearted encouragement when they—cross your fingers—become rich and famous.

148. Turn your driver's license photo session into performance art. Ladies, skip the makeup; men, grow a scraggly beard. Everyone scowl when they say, "Smile!" If you ever get pulled over and the officer compares your grizzled photo to your smiling face, he may assume you've turned your

life around. He might cut you a break. Plus, it's a great conversation starter in airport lines.

149. Never skimp on the shoes. A quality shoe can turn long walks into waltzes. And, someday, try to listen to the greatest ode to shoes ever written, "Quality Shoe," by Mark Knopfler from the outstanding 2002 CD, *The Ragpicker's Dream*.

150. Learn the serene pleasures of fly-fishing a lazy river in the summer. Take a class on how to tie your own bugs so you can stay in touch with the soulful daydreams during winter.

151. Own your own Christmas tree farm. Plant a sample of saplings somewhere in the backyard and harvest one each year when it's time for the holidays. If you don't have the room, ask a friendly farmer if he can spare a few square feet.

152. Ask the local weather expert what they called the jet stream before the advent of jets. Guaranteed, it'll be a stumper of a question. When he or she gives up, tell them the answer: they called it … *wind*.

153. See a movie solo. It feels very liberating.

154. Once a month, give your brain a vigorous workout and call a pompous, opinionated radio host and challenge one of his or her sacred cows.

155. No matter if your life is as colorful as a Salvador Dali painting or the great Dali himself, never walk away from any conversation having said more words than the person to whom you've been talking. Colorful people become more colorful by listening, not yapping.

156. Participate in Take Our Daughters and Sons to Work Day, but don't give your child a sanitized version designed to show how hard you work. If you devote part or most of the day to goofing off, then revel in goofing off.

157. Next time you hear anyone invite you to go out and raise some hell, gently suggest that maybe the world would be better off if we all spent some time trying to lower heaven.

158. He's cheerful, polite, and enjoys laughter. Go ahead and tell people the Pillsbury Dough Boy is among the world's greatest roll models.

159. Break a lull in any conversation by asking if anyone has ever put gloves in their car's glove compartment.

160. Be spiritually colorful like Henry David Thoreau. Shortly before his death on May 6, 1862, the great author and philosopher was asked if he'd made his peace with God. His reply? "I did not know that we had ever quarreled." Live your life at peace with yourself and your Creator.

161. An expectant mother is one of the most marvelous things to behold. If you're expecting, be sure to exploit the condition in order to get free stuff.

Colorful Days Diary

I wish I had a great, big pregnant woman to take to Pirates games. Understand, I don't want anything to do with causing her pregnancy or, gadzooks, for being responsible for the ensuing squaller.

Who needs that?

But the Pittsburgh Pirates are just coming off a great home stand that saw them take two of three from the Major League best

Philadelphia Phillies. PNC Park was packed. It was a great baseball atmosphere.

I wish I could have been there. But I haven't been to a baseball game all year. I still resent the cheapskate owners and the high prices, and the year's been a tumult of family obligations that have vacuumed up all my time and income.

The weekend had me missing the summers when I was at a ballgame at least once a week.

Prior to all the eventual mayhem resulting from my own pregnant wife, I used to attend as many as thirty games a year with my buddies. And what fun we had.

We'd sit there in the stands guzzling beer, profanely jeering the opposition, and spouting just enough real baseball insight to confuse the crowd into thinking we were idiot scouts.

In fact, we might as well have been. My peak baseball attending years coincided with the eighteen-year span involving some of the worst baseball in Pirates history.

Real Pirates idiot scouts were probably just a few sections over acting exactly like we were and confusing fans into thinking they were just drunken fans.

So we had a lot of giddy guy fun.

But I also loved, for different reasons, going with my wife, never more so than when she was great with child.

To many people, professional baseball is boring. I guess to them life is, too.

I find it impossible to mix more than twenty thousand people, an interesting athletic spectacle, and seven-dollar domestic beers and not be entertained. It's all theater.

That's why my wife was such a great, big asset when she had a really great, big, uh, profile.

It always happened on Sundays when the team was giving away crappy souvenirs to kids ten and under.

There were cheap jerseys, batting helmets, team clocks—stuff nobody wants.

Unless it's free.

I remember on this bright Sunday they were giving away tiny Giant Eagle–sponsored Kevin Young souvenir bats. These were miniature foot-long versions of the game-used bats Young swung, but for practical purposes they might as well have been the real thing.

Young couldn't hit a curve ball with a Giant Eagle souvenir bass fiddle.

Still, I felt a craving. I saw the ticket takers distributing the cheesy novelties to the line of dopey kids and thought, *How can I get my hands on one?*

That's when it struck me: I already had a dopey kid of my own. It was just that neither my wife nor I had met her yet.

The ticket taker scanned our tickets and gave a friendly, "Enjoy the game!"

I asked him if I could have a bat.

"Sorry, pal, those are only for kids ten and under."

That's when I pointed at the audacious belly of my eight-month-pregnant wife.

"C'mon!" said the flabbergasted gatekeeper. "The kid's gotta be with you!"

He'd fallen right into my trap.

"Are you telling me life doesn't begin at conception?" I shouted. "This isn't some senseless mass of tissue. It is a child! In fact, it's possible we will enter this game as a couple, but leave before the seventh-inning stretch as a family. She's due any minute!

"Now, I'll be happy to stand here and argue Roe v. Wade with you all day, but I'm not leaving until you give me a lousy bat!"

I felt sort of bad for the guy because he never thought when he'd taken what is generally a happy minimum-wage job that he'd be asked to litigate third-trimester legalities.

But, hey, I wanted that bat.

He gave it to me—and I was careful to ensure that he gave it to me and not my humiliated wife, who later said she would have used it to beat me senseless to the cheers of the exasperated crowd.

I still have that bat. The kid, too.

Sometimes I still pick it up, squeeze it, and think of all the carefree times I had down at the ol' ball game.

It brings back a lot of really great memories. It still means a lot to me.

I'll leave it up to you to decide whether I'm referring here to the kid or the bat.

162. Colorful folks conversation starter: Ask friends if they think Elvis have ever reached and maintained his iconic status if the Presleys had named their son Todd.

163. Start a "Go Green! Run All the Reds!" movement by writing a letter to the local paper advocating motorists start running red lights when no one is near. There are plenty of rural red lights that should not be obeyed as long as no one is coming. It saves gas, saves time, and gives you a little triumph over a machine that cannot reason the way you can.

164. Once a week, take a soulful mile-long walk with a plastic grocery bag. You need not veer, but stoop down and pick up any trash that you'd otherwise have to step over. If you feel like it, go ahead and pick up the nearby trash, too. Some people will think you're a nut tilting at recyclable windmills. Others will think you're inspiring. If anyone asks why you're picking up trash that isn't even yours, tell them the trash might not be yours, but the planet is.

165. Attend a Christmas or Easter service at the oldest church in town.

166. It doesn't matter if it's in the shower by yourself or in a choir surrounded by joyful voices—sing! Sing! Sing!

167. Urge your local zoo to begin hosting weekly giraffe races on the grounds that every contest would be neck and neck.

168. If you have a younger, crankier child who is having a fit, offer the older child one dollar to make a face so funny

the younger one will laugh. If it works, it'll be worth it twice: once when the shrieking stops and then when the two little squabblers bond over the funnies.

169. Give yourself a poor man's massage. Take a golf ball and roll it on the big muscles in your legs for two minutes. It'll release the tension that comes from sitting all day. Then take your shoes off and treat the feet by rolling that golf ball beneath all the pressure points in your aching feet.

170. Surprise the boys in the garage and bring the rental car back free of interior debris and washed to gleaming. It'll give them time for a break and something to talk about the rest of the week.

171. In a crowded mall parking lot with someone tailing you, deliberately pass up a prime spot and go straight to the farthest reaches of the lot. The walk will do you good, and some stranger will skip through the rest of the day bragging about the great spot he or she nailed right next to the front door.

172. If you're within two or three hours of a river town threatened by flooding, take a couple of vacation days, race to the site, and volunteer to bag sand to save the town. Strangers will hug you, the free coffee will never taste better, and you'll feel like a lower case superhero, especially if you don't tell your coworkers what you did on your vacation.

173. Try to compose a Bible-worthy proverb, such as, "Fools pray for money and get nothing. The righteous pray for wisdom and need nothing." It's not in the Bible, but there's still a chance it'll make Bible II.

174. Every two years or so, spend a night nominating your spouse and vice versa to be family president. Make impassioned nominating speeches about each other's better points in front of the kids. Have them vote to see who gets to be family president for the next term. If the winner goes power mad, get together with the kids and start a petty impeachment drive.

175. Always correct the misrepresentation that so-and-so is a "rock star" of whatever nonmusical realm in which they enjoy some petty renown. Point out that calling anyone in any field that doesn't involve drugs, groupies, and ear-blistering electric guitars a rock star is a blazing insult to historic excessives like Keith Richards, Tommy Lee, and Keith Moon. Guys on financial shows, for instance, aren't rock stars in their respective fields. They're simply dorks with shticks.

176. Use talk of routine death at the dinner table for a fun and engaging way to educate kids on the joys of colorful living.

Colorful Days Diary

I put a moratorium on boring dinner deaths the other night after yet another old neighbor lady passed away in her sleep.

It's not that I'm opposed to morbid death talk at dinner. On the contrary, I've always considered myself a death connoisseur. I enjoy lively talks about death and dying.

As a young newspaper reporter, I was daily immersed in the grisly ends of strangers. I've seen with my own eyes the mangled bodies of gunshot victims, sidewalk suicide splatters, and hapless casualties of no-win confrontations with runaway trucks.

Their scarred corpses haunt my dreams. I wonder about the searing pain and the fateful recognition that death was imminent. And I invariably put myself in their doomed shoes, hands raised in futile defense the instant before the pin hits the shell.

It's not death I mind; it's boredom.

And our seven-year-old daughter shares those impulses. So the other night when my wife said the neighbor lady died, our daughter was naturally curious. How'd she die? What happened?

"She was old," my wife said. "She died in her sleep. Very peaceful."

It was maybe the eighth old lady who'd died in her sleep this year. If you're looking for a tidy, peaceful death, become an old lady in my neighborhood and just bide your time.

I could sense our daughter was disappointed. I set my fork down and wiped my mouth with my napkin. "Look, I'm tired of all these old ladies dying in their sleep," I said to my wife. "The next time some old lady passes away, you make damn sure you have a good story to tell us. It's not going to make her any less dead if she was eaten by a bear or struck by lightning. And we'll all enjoy our dinners a little bit more."

So recently we've had wonderful dinner conversations about Mrs. Miller who was struck by a meteor while she was gardening; Mrs. Peterson, who died heroically trying to save her kidnapped husband from Colombian rebels; and poor old Mrs. Benson, who was killed trying to retrieve her wedding ring from the cranky wood chipper in the backyard.

I have absolutely no fear of death as long as it doesn't have to hurt.

I probably spend a lot of time thinking about dying because I spend so much time thinking about living. I really enjoy my life and know it's finite. We're all born the same way, but death's a real crapshoot. Even mean, rich people can die grisly, untimely deaths, and we all feel a little bit better about ourselves when something like that happens.

It's one of the most fair things about this confounding and often unfair life.

Ideally, I'd like to live to be about ninety, stumble drunk out of a friendly tavern, and get hit by a bus. I want the bus to be traveling so fast that bystanders will swear they saw my soul shoot out of my body, bound straight for heaven. And that my soul wasn't wearing any pants.

But I'm guessing it's most likely to happen in a movie theater where I'll be gunned down by some rude, yapping kids who don't like being shushed by an old man who feels it's his duty to police the audience so everyone can hear the witty dialogue animating what I guess will be *Shrek 19*.

No matter what happens, I've started a family tradition that when I do go, it'll be something that'll entertain my darling daughters.

My wife: "Kids, I've got bad news. Your father was killed today. He was struck by a meteor while fighting Colombian rebels with a wood chipper. His body fell off the mountain he was climbing and landed in shark-infested waters just as the nearby volcanic island erupted …"

Sure, some of that might hurt, but it ought to give me bragging rights when I run into all those old neighbor ladies who—yawn—died in their sleep.

177. Ask jarringly innocent questions—"Could it be the spark plugs?"—of tech people during the interminable time waiting for the busted computer to reboot. Not only will it shake them out of their stupors, it'll let them understand that they really need to keep things simple when trying to solve your infernal computer problems.

178. Rent a classic made-for-TV miniseries—*Lonesome Dove, Roots*—during the bleakest weeks of winter and watch the episodes in the evenings, two hours at a time. It'll give you something to look forward to each day.

179. Use cookbooks to get good ideas, but remember, there are no referees in the kitchen. If the recipe says use 1/4 teaspoon of oregano and you like oregano, put all you want in. It won't ruin it; it'll season it to your tastes. Recipe measurements are merely suggestions.

180. Know the location of a good vinyl record store in town and stop by once in a while. Find some old favorites, read the liner notes, hold the vinyl, and remember the crackling magic of the first time you heard the needle hit the groove. Ask where you can still find a good turntable.

181. Point out that in movies, most cars don't have rearview mirrors. But they still have the little window dot that used to secure the star-obscuring mirror.

182. Learn to skate well enough so you can enjoy a wintry day on a frozen pond with a stick and a puck. It's pure joy.

183. Always challenge conventional wisdom. If the conventional wisdom is so wise, why is so much of the world such a mess?

184. Tell friends you're in favor of a color blind society, but worry what that just result will mean to our nation's sock drawers.

185. Be respectful of vegetarians, but ask them how they square their diet with this bit of bumper sticker wisdom: "If God had intended man to be vegetarians, why did He make animals out of meat?"

186. You probably receive an occasional brochure from a local community college. Give it a look and take a class on something offbeat like pottery or woodworking. It'll get you out of the house, you'll learn a new hobby, and you'll make some new friends.

187. Don't let the gloomy insurance industry fool you: a child's birth, a towering Redwood and a beautiful sunset are all acts of God, too.

188. Talk like a CB-radio-jawing trucker every time you take a long road trip. Say things to your passengers like, "Breaker, breaker, one-niner, what's your twenty?" If you need to brush up on CB talk, rent the great Burt Reynolds and Jackie Gleason movie, *Smokey and the Bandit*. It's hilarious.

189. Try brewing your own beer or making your own wine. It'll probably be awful, but it will be fun. And—who knows?—it might turn out to be great.

190. Most of us spend our entire lives staring straight ahead. Try some eye exercises. Roll your eyes. Move them to the left. Move them to the right. The exercises will strengthen the muscles controlling eye movements and, yes, looking out the side of your eye is kind of sexy.

191. Did you know a regulation No. 2 pencil like the kind you used in school contains enough pencil lead to write a straight unbroken line for thirty-five miles? Colorful people do.

192. Love your loved ones so much you love 'em even when they leave you alone.

Colorful Days Diary

The girls cried two years ago when they pulled out of the driveway for five days away with Mommy and their aunt. "We're gonna miss you, Daddy!" the older one wailed as the car rumbled on down the street.

As soon as the car was out of sight, I remember doing a euphoric little jig. It'll forever confound me how the three people I love more than any others can make me so ecstatically happy by leaving me all alone.

The scene will be repeated tomorrow at 8:00 a.m. For the first night in more than two years, I'll have the house to myself. No wife. No kids. No cares.

That means I have fewer than eighteen hours to invent from scratch a machine that can stop time. The girls will be gone about thirty-six hours. If I could stretch that period to, say, a week, I'd do it. That would give me time to do all the nothing I won't be able to squeeze into tomorrow and Sunday.

And when I say nothing, I mean nothing. I'm not going rake the yard, put up the screens, or dust any of the household items that'll be gathering dust through a weekend of peaceful inactivity.

If they'd present a trophy for what guys like me do on rare weekends like this, the golden figure would be seated in a recliner with a remote in one hand, a beer in the other, and a bowl of pretzels cradled in his paunchy lap.

There are many good family men who want to spend their every waking moment with their families. Any separation freights them with a sadness they wear like a cloak.

I'm not one of them.

My family reminds me of an old Dan Hicks country song, "How Can I Miss You When You Won't Go Away?"

Part of the problem is I'm just not brave enough to be lazy. My wife works very hard to keep the house and the kids looking great. So if she walks in a room and I'm—heaven forbid—just sitting there, I feel guilty. In fact, I often pop up out of my seat so the motion will confuse her into thinking I'm just finishing or about to embark on some tedious household chore.

If I had more time, I'd have all the boys over for cigars and beers. This is another thing I never get to do. We have a really great guy house with a big back porch that overlooks the woods and a babbling mountain creek. The woods are a great place for beer drinkers to stumble about and decorate the rocks once our bodies are done with the beers, and that's a perennially fun guy thing to do.

But having the boys over would cut into my sitting time. I intend to be the first couch potato so sedentary that he lapses into a persistent vegetative state.

I plan on watching one John Wayne movie (probably *Red River*), one Rolling Stones concert DVD, a replay of the Steelers Super Bowl victory, the hilarious guy movies *Animal House* and *Hot Fuzz*, and about sixteen hours of NCAA tournament basketball.

I've made some delicious seafood soup, plan on having at least one pizza, and plan on grilling a juicy steak.

The whole time, I'll feel like I'm the luckiest guy in the world.

And on Sunday evening, I'll once again be confounded as to how a guy who can be so blissfully happy when he's left all alone can be surprised by a jolt of euphoria at the sound of his three girls storming back into the house.

193. Plato said, "Never discourage anyone ... who continually makes progress, no matter how slow." Smart guy, that Plato. If you see someone, no matter how misshapen, walking or running to improve their fitness, give them the thumbs-up and say, "Way to go. Keep it up!"

194. Sign off your letters with something distinctive. Instead of "Regards," or "Sincerely," try something like, "Keep on truckin'!"

195. Commit to memory at least one great quote from as many famous people as you can. For instance, "Evil is not driven out, but crowded out." —Martin Luther King, Jr.

196. Maybe a rabbit's foot won't work for you. Try other good luck charms. In Brazil, members of certain tribes wear freeze-dried piranha around their necks for good luck.

197. Let your spouse, on his or her birthday, behave just like an impetuous child. Say that you'll grant any wish that begins with "I want ..." Specify not to get too greedy because your birthday will be an "I want" day, too!

198. Become an organ donor (www.organdonor.gov) and let everyone know of your charitable intentions. Encourage loved ones to do the same.

199. Take a long walk in the woods. Carry along a turkey-gobbler and scratch out some mating calls. You might attract some turkeys. Or you might attract an interesting person who will enhance your stroll. If you dare do it during turkey season, wear lots and lots of fluorescent orange.

200. Eat a green apple and cucumber salad while either a green apple or cucumber candle burns nearby. These two scents have proven to reduce anxiety and boost your mood.

201. It'll all be a lot easier on you if you remember that the only thing we can do to remotely influence the way people treat us is to be considerate about the way we treat people.

202. Flatter your self-esteem whenever anyone suggests you resemble someone else. Go ahead and assume the look-alike is gorgeous.

Colorful Days Diary

The two looked like what we in high school used to call "burnouts"—dingy, cloudy-eyed inhabitants of my high school's smoking area.

And consider that for a moment: at one time, many of us attended high school in a not-too-distant age when enlightened school administrators actually had designated areas where teenagers so disposed could go out and smoke their butts off.

When you think about it, it was an age of great liberty, one the Founding Fathers would surely have approved of, even as the Founding Surgeon Generals gave their scolding disapproval.

But back to the burnouts. They were standing and, yes, smoking outside of a local tobacco shop while I was approaching during my afternoon stroll.

"Mr. Rockton?" one of them called out as I was about twenty paces away. "Is that you, Mr. Rockton?"

I turned around and saw no one. They thought I was Rockton, and for a still-lingering instant, I was wishing I was.

Rockton's a great name. Surely the guy had to be some kind of butt-kicking private eye—*Rockton, P.I.!*—and for purposes of clarity, I'm talking about anatomical butts, not nicotine-laced ones.

"Aren't you Mr. Rockton? The teacher?" he asked.

"Nope, sorry, fellas. Wrong guy," I said.

"Oh, sorry. You look just like him."

Now I'm dying to find Rockton.

We are forever at the mercy of those whom we resemble.

If someone tells a beautiful woman she resembles the lovely Kate Winslet, it's an enduring compliment that'll brighten her every day. Years from now, grandchildren on her knee, she'll be flipping through old photos and telling the little sprouts that strangers used to tell her she was a ringer for the ravishing Winslet.

It won't matter even a tiny bit when the bored kids say, "Who the hell's Kate Winslet?"

But tell the same woman she looks like drug-ravaged crooner du jour and she'll dive for her iPhone to start researching face transplants.

Is Rockton handsome and dashing, the way I picture myself? What if he's a pointy-headed nerd?

I think it would be a great twilight zone sort of gift if, for just one afternoon, we could see ourselves the way others, particularly strangers, see us.

I guess I've always had a chip on my broad, muscular shoulders because everyone always said my older, taller brother looked just like Tom Selleck of *Magnum, P.I.* They said I looked like I never got enough sleep.

I gaze in the mirror—and I do an unhealthy amount of that—and see a rakish face with a dashing devil-may-care smile. I say out loud, "Why, if it isn't Rhett Butler! The ladies in the parlor are breathlessly awaiting your arrival!" Then I turn serious, searing the mirror with a look the romance novelists call penetrating. "When people see this face," I say, "they must immediately think of Gregory Peck in *To Kill a Mockingbird* or *The Guns of Navarone*."

I do this almost daily for nearly ten minutes until the exasperated mirror finally blurts out, "Would you get the hell out of the bathroom and for heaven's sake try to earn a little money, you vain ass!"

So, of course, I'm nervous about someday meeting my Rockton doppelgänger.

I told a good buddy of mine about it. Well, he knows Rockton and sees the resemblance. Turns out my twin's a retired art teacher at the local elementary school. He hunts, too.

That's encouraging. With art, he has a sensitive side, and I hear that's a plus with the ladies in the parlor, but the hunter bit gives him a rugged outdoorsy edge. The guy's probably good in a bar fight.

He's a teacher, too, and I have a great and enduring affection for people who devote their lives to educating our youth, and that even goes for all those raging tyrants who tried to fill my head with so much math and crap all those years ago.

Sounds like Rockton's a great guy.

That's good. It reduces the chances I might one day get dragged into the police station and shoved in front of some trembling crime victim whose addled brain will instantly cause her to shriek, "That's him! That's the Latrobe Flasher!"

On the contrary, if he ever does an anonymous good deed, I might get credit, which I'll certainly hog.

But none of that matters to me. I could care less if Rockton's a good guy or a demonic, pants-dropping fiend.

I just hope he's gorgeous.

203. Take a good look at your shoes in the morning. That's the last you should see of them all day. Look up! Look around! Notice things you've never noticed before.

204. Get lost in an unfamiliar neighborhood. Admire the homes, the landscapes. Try to find a new restaurant to enjoy or a time-saving shortcut to beat the traffic.

205. Make two bookmarks from long locks of your children's hair. Keep one for yourself. Give the other to Grandpa.

206. The people of Yuma, Arizona, refer to themselves as Yumans. Make it a bucket-list point to enter a 5K there so you can say you're a member of the Yuman race and have a T-shirt to prove it.

207. Take deep breaths through your nose while in the shower. It'll clear out your sinuses and give the lungs a good steaming.

208. Take an afternoon to enjoy a local art gallery featuring some of the works of the masters like Picasso, Van Gogh, or Pissarro. When no one's looking, shuck off your shoes, run as fast as you can, and see how far you can slide in your stocking feet.

209. Turn down the volume of the "hollerdays." Dedicate one night a week prior to Christmas to sitting in silence and reading old Christmas stories aloud to the family in front of a fire. Softly.

210. Avoid using too many *italicized phrases* in one paragraph *lest* it make readers *see-sick*.

211. Set the alarm clock for the wee hours anytime the newscasters announce—yippee!—there will be a meteor shower and clear skies at 3:00 a.m.

212. Don't be so skeptical about compliments. If someone tells you you're wonderful, don't hem and haw. Just be gracious and say thanks. Because chances are they are correct. You are wonderful.

Colorful Days Diary

Fresh evidence that marriage is a terrific antidote to excessive ego was delivered recently when my wife and I met friends out for drinks.

I'd been surprised and pleased, as I always am, to find Cheryl had become an avid reader of my www.EightDaysToAmish.com blog. Really, with as busy as we all are, I'm surprised and pleased anyone takes time to read things like rat poison warning labels before they splash it all over the kids' breakfast cereal.

Time's precious. Reading a pointless blog like mine seems like the height of frivolity, the fiscal equivalent of lighting cigars with hundred dollar bills.

So I said hello by thanking her effusively.

Well, in poker terms, she saw my effusiveness and raised it. Through the roof.

"I love your blog! You're great! Your stuff is so funny! I especially like it when . . ."

I began to settle in for a good long preen that I was sure would conclude with her saying when she reads my blog aloud the sad become happy, the sick become well, the stupid miraculously become smart.

But my wife jumped in and cut her right off: "So what have you guys been up to?"

What?

You'd think a wife would enjoy hearing someone gush over her husband. After all, this is a woman who often hears me monologue for hours about my many career failures and everlasting inability to earn a buck.

Let me tell you, that's one little soliloquy she never interrupts, much less contradicts.

I turned to her in amazement and said, "How rude! She might just be getting started. Why interrupt her when she's gushing about how great I am? Please, Cheryl, continue and speak into this handy megaphone . . ."

But the moment had passed, ruined by a typical spouse ever vigilant against a significant other feeling a tad too superior.

Of course, her reaction was perfectly reasonable. Who among us doesn't prefer the company of the humble to the arrogant, the Tebow to the Trump?

Our spouses are intimate accountants of our flaws. They know our strengths and weaknesses, our fears, our failures and what about us is truly admirable.

I'll never forget the night Val told me one of my most endearing characteristics is a stubborn ability to maintain supreme self-confidence without any foundational achievement.

At least I think she said endearing. She may have said exasperating.

I remain humble about my ability to be a good listener.

Either way, she's right.

Believe me, you don't want to spend an afternoon mirror shopping with a guy like me.

That's why what I'm about to say next may seem surprising.

I'm eager for people to say nice things about me, but immediately feel like fleeing the room once they do.

Had Cheryl gone on any longer, I'd have instinctively begun wondering if she was either fresh from rehab or in desperate need of rehab.

I guess it's because -- with the exception of touchy-feely places like Southern California -- we live in a society that is utterly resistant to compliments.

Tell a woman she's beautiful and she'll immediately dash off five self-perceived flaws to counter the contention.

Part of that reaction is healthy. None of us wants to give the impression of being too full of ourselves. It's obnoxious.

But what's wrong with graciously acknowledging the parts of ourselves that other people admire?

Is there too much pressure to be beautiful? To be kind? To be wonderful?

The great Keb' Mo' wrote the 2004 song, "I'm Amazing," a tune that without conceit says we all have warmth and worth and ought to celebrate ourselves and one another. The relevant lyrics are worthy of sharing.

I'm amazing! I'm incredible!
I'm a miracle and a dream come true!
I'm marvelous! I'm beautiful!
Guess what?
So are you.

This hard world would be a little bit easier if we all were a little more generous with the heartfelt compliments to one another and a little more forgiving of ourselves and others.

Cheryl is right.

I am great.

So's she.
Guess what?
And so are you!
This post?
I gotta be honest, I think it kind of sucked.

213. Research a worthwhile charitable organization to ensure it will spend your money wisely, and then faithfully begin to donate—not only your money but also your time.

214. Listen to the school closings on days when bitter winter keeps the school buses off the roads. If they call the name of your old school district, go to work late. Or, what the heck, blow the whole day off and stay home and watch cartoons in front of the fire.

215. Stop using speed dial and exercise your brain by committing numbers to memory. You'll be grateful you did when you're a senior citizen searching for the car keys.

216. Learn to make your own salsa.

217. Carry a bottle of Tabasco sauce with you to liven up even the most mundane meals.

218. The math nerds will point out its inaccuracies, but colorful people will enjoy it if you tell them that if Don McLean had written "American Pi," the last lyric might have been "… this'll be the day that I die that I die that I die that I …"

219. With your sweetheart as a willing accomplice, sneak a bottle of wine, two glasses, and a corkscrew into a long matinee.

220. Who says you can't have doughnuts for dinner? Once in a while, reverse the order of your meals. Have dinner for

breakfast, breakfast for dinner, and lunch, well, there's nothing wrong with having lunch in the middle of the day.

221. Try and go to a store or coffee shop in the morning that will allow you the opportunity to say a friendly, "Hey!" to at least three people, thus ensuring you're bound to have a real heyday.

222. Traffic delays are an inevitable part of our daily commute. Plan for them by adding extra time, keeping something to read in the car, and vowing not to get angry about something that's completely out of your hands. In short, don't be a carmudgeon.

223. Someday, just for the fun of it, stand on a busy street corner and bark into the cell phone, "No! No! No! The incision should be made behind the left ear! The left ear!"

224. Two things every good home needs on every floor: a dictionary and a back scratcher. That's a dictionary and a back scratcher for the basement, a dictionary and a back scratcher for the first floor, and a dictionary and a back scratcher for the second floor. It's okay if one of your back scratchers is the two-legged kind.

225. Always include the honorary salutation "Rev." before your name whenever you're filling out subscriptions or registration cards. You'll be amazed at the fawning service you get.

Colorful Days Diary

The Sierra Club refers to me with the honorific "Judge Chris Rodell." The noble lifesavers at Doctors Without Borders address me with collegial charity as "Dr. Rodell." And it would take a miracle of biblical proportions for me to respond with the generosity deserving of all the Democratic Party affiliates who write beseeching "The Reverend Rodell" for a contribution.

If you took all the mailing lists for every left-leaning, tree-hugging, bound-to-help-the-helpless organizations in the world and rolled them into one, the sum distillation would be one of the most accomplished men in the world. And that would be me. After a lifetime of willful indolence, finally, a man Mom can be proud of.

See, being Mr. Chris Rodell hasn't exactly worked out for me. No one treats me with anything more than the most perfunctory courtesies.

That's why I hesitated in 2004 when a donation to the Democratic Party required me to check a title. "Dr." felt like a reach. "Mrs." would have worked with the wussy unisex name my parents freighted me with at birth, but I wasn't ready for the possible lifestyle change it might invite and I would have needed a whole new wardrobe.

So I stared at the heavenly option, "Rev." Remember, 2004 was when Karl Rove and the Republicans frequently claimed they'd been anointed by the Almighty to divinely solve all the world's problems. I decided to do my part to close the God gap. For my title, I checked "Rev."

Right away, the new title led to more telephonic respect. One agent for the party called and said, "Reverend Rodell? I'm sooo sorry to bother you, but we really need the help of upstanding community men like you if we're going to win in November. Can we count on your support and influence?"

By all means. I dashed off a check for fifty dollars, and the 2006 Congressional elections wound up being an electoral landslide, coincidentally, perhaps. Soon, my name began to sift through the other left-leaning mailing lists. I could sense in their tones that the callers' postures improved when they dialed a holy man like myself.

I liked it.

Of course, there was the inevitable misstep. During the recent Pennsylvania primary, I was besieged by calls from party activists. I lost my patience and reverted back to my Mr. Rodell temper.

"Look," I told one caller, "I'm gettin' sick of all these (and I'm paraphrasing here) gol-danged calls. Leave me alone!"

The solicitor let the silence sink in for two beats before saying, "Rev. Rodell?"

"Uh, yes?"

"You should be nicer. People expect more from someone like you."

He was right. People look up to those involved in pastoral professions, and as I'm finding out, even to ones who pretend to be. If I'm going to be Rev. Rodell, there are certain standards I need to uphold.

So I vowed to make myself a better person, at least in terms of titles. Besides "Judge," "Dr.," "Father," and "Esq.," I was pleased to feel an ecumenical surge of pride when UNICEF bestowed upon me, for one hundred dollars, the title of "Rabbi."

I doubt the unfortunates in Myanmar or China will care whether or not Rabbi Rodell is concerned about their plight, but it might open some eyes if, say, he extends a financial olive branch to help aid Palestinian orphans.

Either way, it's likely I'll one day leave a remarkable obituary for my survivors to admire. And maybe one day I'll live up to the reputation of the guy all those money-seeking callers believe me to be.

It's something you might want to consider next time someone seeks a contribution from you.

Of course, that's just my opinion. You can take it or leave it.

After all, despite what you might infer from my credentials, I'm really not a preachy kind of guy.

226. No matter where you're headed, take long, robust strides. Both literally and figuratively.

227. Make a Google scrapbook about a loved one. Type their name—say, Mark Johnson—into the www.google.com search engine. Then make printouts of all the things "Mark Johnson" has done. For instance, "Mark Johnson wins an Olympic medal," or "Mark Johnson saves three from fire!" or "Mark Johnson convicted of forgery." Give it to your loved one on a special holiday and read "his" exploits aloud.

228. Tear up some sheets of paper and keep the shreds in a cup on your desk. Next time you or someone in your office learns of some spontaneous good news, toss the homemade confetti in the air.

229. Every day, if you can, do the same number of pushups, squats, or a comparative exercise as you had candles on your most recent birthday cake. Do no more, no less. If you start early enough, twenty pushups a day won't be that tough, adding one a year will be a cinch, and the lifelong benefits will be startling.

230. Refer to boutique urban lodging places that used to be notorious brothels as "ho'tels."

231. It's so cliché, you'll be embarrassed if anyone catches you doing it, so be discreet. Whenever you're fortunate enough to enjoy a long sea voyage, put a note in a bottle. Ask the prospective recipient to send you a small souvenir from the finder's hometown. Include a twenty-dollar bill, cross your fingers, and heave the sealed bottle into the waves. Who knows? Maybe someday, maybe years later, you'll get a pleasant surprise in the mail.

232. Always stay for at least two drinks anytime you walk into a bar filled with strangers. Ordering one and leaving makes you look like a tourist. Ordering a second round friendlies up the locals and leads to warm banter with people who are always eager to talk to a stranger.

233. Colorful conversation starter: Ask friends how come if none of us has ever seen, much less flown on a non-military black jet, how did the term "jet-black" become so instantly informative?

234. Attempt great, near-impossible tasks throughout your life and never give up or give in. Even if you forever fail, and you may, the attempting is what's important.

235. Say "Cheese Whiz!" Experts say speaking the words leaves the facial muscles in a relaxed and confident position, making people more eager to do your bidding.

236. Learn common sense from uncommon people. For instance, the world's most traveled man, the late John Clouse, said he always packed light and took socks, underwear, and an old toothbrush that he could simply throw away rather than cart home.

237. Plant some mint in your backyard or in a cozy windowsill garden box. Tend to it until the first weekend of May, when you can enjoy it with some bourbon in a mint julep while you're watching the Kentucky Derby. Then put a leaf or two in your iced tea for the rest of the summer.

238. If you hear a stranger sneeze, always follow up with a "God bless you," even if it's to yourself. God'll get it.

239. Go ahead and get a pedicure. Spa guests typically opt for a back massage, but a pedicure treats the most ill-attended and abused part of the body: it treats the feet.

Colorful Days Diary

She brought the sundae out on a little tray. There were big scoops of strawberry, chocolate, and vanilla ice cream, and an oozy river of creamy caramel. How could I resist? I did what any red-blooded American male would do.

I dunked my big cracked, calloused, and stinking feet right in the whole gooey mess and began wiggling my toes.

I was at the cloud-clinging Wintergarden Spa at the Wintergreen Resort in the Blue Ridge Mountains, a heavenly perch so elevated that you're actually looking down upon the tops of hawks. My spa options included the standard sports massage and manicure, but I decided to treat the most abused and maltreated part of my entire body.

I decided to treat the feet. I was there to get my first pedicure, something men rarely did and now are doing in growing numbers. The International SPA Association reported that 22 percent of men who go to spas do so to get their toes done.

If that's true, they're not doing any bragging about it. Anecdotally, I've talked to many men who enjoy spas, but none who've confessed to getting a pedicure. Perhaps it's because men are hardwired to believe, as I've been instructed by my wife, that "feet should be smelled not seen."

She may be prejudiced by near-constant exposure to mine. They're everything I try not to be.

I try to comport myself as a gentleman. I wear nice clothes, exercise, and address people with refined manners. But if I am a gentleman, my feet are outlaw bikers. They're scarred, mean-looking rascals. Tattoo-like bruises mar several stubbed toes, and one ragged nail makes the left foot look as if it's walking around brandishing a drawn knife and looking for a fight. If you saw them by themselves strolling down the sidewalk without the rest of me to soften their impression, you'd cross the street.

But despite their haggard appearance, I've always considered them to be a pair of sissies. They whimper barefoot on a freshly mown lawn and practically shriek out loud when subjected to things like hot beach sand or poolside concrete.

Lately, however, I've been immersing myself in foot literature. There was a great Adam Sternbergh article in the April 28, 2008, edition of *New York* magazine that reads: "You Walk Wrong: It took 4 million years of evolution to perfect the human foot. But we're wrecking it with every step we take."

The article says our mistreatment of our feet leads to back and joint pain that's become unnecessarily endemic to growing old.

Maybe it's time to give more healthcare priority to the feet. That's why I opted for the Wintergarden Spa's $75 Sole Sundae pedicure, "designed for the ice cream lover in all of us. First soak in your favorite flavor of ice cream. Next enjoy a scrub in a refreshing sherbet flavor, followed by a choice of foot mask in chocolate, caramel, or marshmallow. Top off this Sundae with Body Icing infused with Shea Butter and vitamins that will leave your appetite wanting more."

The sundae treatment included soothing elements that mimicked ice cream in texture and scent.

"You can't eat it, but it always makes me hungry," said Ashley, the pretty blonde pedicurist, as she began to massage my tootsies after they'd been soaking for ten minutes in a warm pool of strawberry-scented water.

It didn't take long for my feet to fall in love with Ashley. No one had ever treated them the way she did, and for the first time, I began to understand men for whom the foot is fetishized, and wished I'd found a woman who felt that way. Ashley rubbed them, massaged them with manicured fingers, and charmed them when she daintily turned away to cough, rather than risk offending a foot. It was very sweet.

And heavenly. I can't get my wife to rub my back after I've spent an afternoon chopping firewood she'll use to comfort herself on bitter winter days. There's no way she'd consider rubbing the ugly feet as a means of giving me physical pleasure. Heck, getting her to rub anything to give me physical pleasure usually takes some gentle persuading, a lit candle, and a nice bottle of cabernet.

Not Ashley. She was into it.

"My friends are always asking me, 'How can you rub some of those ugly feet?'" she said. "I tell them I can rub any foot that's been soaked clean. But you have very nice feet. I can tell you take care of them."

Beneath the dark chocolate scrub, I could tell the boys were blushing. They were unaccustomed to such flattery.

She also shared some fascinating feet facts. For instance, pregnant women are discouraged from getting a vigorous foot massage or reflexology, the practice that believes all the bodily constitutions are legislated through precise nerves in our feet and hands.

"They say touching a pregnant woman's ankle right … here …"—Ooh! Ahhh!—"can cause her to go right into labor."

Nothing so dramatic happened when she touched me there, a reassuring sign for a man who was still a little self-conscious about the procedure.

For me, the foot massage was a heavenly revelation. It was better than any back massage I'd ever gotten. Sure, the back has its burdens, but when you think about it rationally, what part of the body undergoes more daily punishment than feet?

I confess, too, that the encounter left me feeling playful enough that Ashley and I agreed to another act of intimacy that, try as I might, I couldn't conceal from my wife and daughters. And then I strode out of there on refreshed feet, still a red-blooded American male confident in his stride and the future of his feet.

A red-blooded American male with five toenails alternately painted Disco Inferno Pink and five colored a boldly cerulean Blue Me Away.

240. To heck with drinking the stuff. Boutique bottled water is too expensive to guzzle. Instead, buy some old-fashioned ice trays and use the premium water to make ice. It'll enrich any cocktail and makes a better story at the parties.

241. Whether it's clothes, jewelry, or office equipment, you can't go wrong investing in yourself. That goes for your savings accounts, too.

242. Play a game of imaginary Ping-Pong with a child and, c'mon, no matter how well you play, let the kid win. Then dramatically pout while the winner gloats. Works just as well with a suitably immature and playful adult friend.

243. Learn yoga. It's as punishing a workout as you can hope for, and it'll sooth the soul while it sustains the body.

244. Encourage others to try adult education on the grounds that there aren't nearly enough educated adults.

245. To heck with big sunken "cement ponds" owned by folks like the Trumps and the Clampetts. Keep a simple kiddie pool in your backyard to lie down in on scorching days so you can revel in the belly-deep cool. You won't look like royalty, but you'll feel like it.

246. While others are enjoying casual Fridays, try on retro-fashion Fridays. Select a decade and celebrate some of the dandier fashions of those iconic years. Not only will you be different, in a few years, you'll appear to be a trendsetter when those fashions come roaring back.

247. Help eliminate road rage and save the environment. One of the best ways to ease daily stress is to live near where you work. The AAA recommends living within three miles of your place of work. Works even better if you can walk there.

248. Slow down. Physicists calculate the world is spinning at a rate of 1,038 miles per hour. That should be fast enough for everyone on board.

249. Celebrate your incompetence. If you make a real sad hash out of a garage project—say, building a simple cabinet—give the whole thing to a neighbor kid on the grounds that if it looks like it was constructed by a seven-year-old, it ought to be owned by one. Then start over and learn from your mistakes.

250. Try your best to get the grammar correct, but don't be judgmental about typos by others or yourself. We're all typing too much, too fast. Mistakes are bound to happen.

Colorful Days Diary

I was a cocky kid fresh out of Ohio University, the top journalism school in the country. Armed with my degree and mastery of a diabolical herd-thinning challenge called the English Proficiency Test, I was going to dazzle the stalwarts at the Nashville Banner.

I remember it was deadline chaos. Nerves were taut, tensions high. They needed the unflappable flash to write a chunk of tight copy to explain a page-one feature picture.

The grizzled old editor raised his voice above the din and yelled, "Get me The Kid!"

It was the moment I'd been waiting for my whole life.

"Kid, we need someone to write some snappy explanation that will have readers jumping out of their seats. Can you send me some sizzle?"

I should explain here I'm overdramatizing this whole story. No one's ever called me "The Kid," I've never been cocky, and I'm always far from the fray whenever challenges arise. Then, as now, when the going got tough, I'd get going to the men's room to hide while I filled out my football pools.

But you get the gist. I was summoned to compose an extended cutline for a big page-one story.

And I thought I did a bang-up job. So I was dumbfounded after the story went to press and the editor, a kind and gentle man, summoned me to say, "Chris, there's a typo in your cutline."

I was devastated. I don't recall the word. Let's say it was "imbecile" and I spelled it "imbassile," thus becoming the first writer to make an ass out of himself while adding an ass to a word.

What's important here is my reaction. I said, "Well, at least it was surrounded by a lot of other properly spelled words."

I instinctively tried to cover my, er, rear by minimizing my error. Really, it was brilliant. The Kid back then had a lot of moxie.

I bring all this up because I want to endorse a stealth movement I've noticed taking hold among people who type: typos, schmypos.

With all our smartphones, Facebook messages, and e-mails, the stigma against casual typos is being buried beneath an avalanche of other properly spelled words.

I say it's about time. I've labored for nearly three decades under the tyranny of the typo.

Blame it on the aforementioned English Proficiency Test at Ohio University.

The test sounds like something conservative presidential candidates want to impose on the people who cross our borders to clean our malls, landscape our McMansions, and harvest our salad crops.

In fact, it was one of those tests that educators inflict on students to frighten them out of their stupors, the lesson being that, hey, this is serious stuff. You're going to be entering a professional world where one careless typo could cost you your job.

Well, no, it couldn't. Maybe a thousand of them could, but only if you're a jerk and the boss is looking for a reason to bounce you.

But writing news stories isn't exactly guard duty at Gitmo. No one's going to die if you put the commas after the conjunctions.

I'm tickled to see smartphone messages appear with the tagline, "Sent from my smurt phone. Please exuse tipos."

I'm thinking I ought to banner that beneath everything I write.

Because mistakes will be made. I welcome when readers point out a mistake, especially when the wording is senselessly mangled. Please feel free to do so as long as you do so in a way that doesn't hurt The Kid's feelings.

But let's not restrict our eagerness to joyfully communicate for fear someone's going to criticize us for minor grammatical mistakes.

Really, anymore it's just not that big a deel.

251. Contribute to history. Find a political candidate for state or national office and send them five dollars toward winning their seat. Then hold them to their promises.

252. Try not to let it get you down knowing that someday rich people are going to get to age more slowly than the rest of us by spending the majority of their time vacationing on Mars.

253. At a fancy restaurant, run your finger atop the mouth-moistened rim of a wine glass. It'll make a sonorous

ringing sound. If anyone asks, tell them the sound and technique is similar to the one invented by Benjamin Franklin's glass armonica, an instrument so melodious that Mozart, Strauss, and Beethoven all composed music specifically to take advantage of its dulcet sounds. Do it once and your companion and other guests will be mildly impressed. Do it more than once and everyone will think you're annoying.

254. Buy some foreign language software and learn a new language on the morning commute. Dream of taking a vacation in the country where you can speak your new language.

255. Calculate the age you feel based on other planets from around our galaxy. For instance, if you're forty-five here on the third rock from the sun and feel youthful, tell people you're about twenty-four in Mars years. That's the earth equivalent of how long it takes the red planet to poke around the sun. But if you've slept poorly and wake up feeling weak and fatigued, tell people you're feeling Venusian, or about seventy-three.

256. Be Napoleonic. He only opened his mail once a month, sure the passage of time would resolve nearly every issue. Resist the urge to constantly check your smartphone.

257. You can be a person of pious faith who believes God created heaven and earth and still tickle your intellect by wondering who or what created God.

258. Once a month, eat only circular things for breakfast, lunch, and dinner. That means doughnuts, burgers, and pizza—with pepperoni!—will dominate the meals. If someone scolds, saying it's an unhealthy diet, challenge them to come up with something more well-rounded.

259. Challenge the language. Ask, as Galileo certainly would, if a dog pound weighs more than a cat pound.

260. Call the game "Three Things." On a long drive, ask each other to list three of anything. Maybe three favorite movies, three favorite songs, etc. Then make the categories more fun and challenging. Three favorite things to do with a chicken (fry, roast, grill with a beer can stuck up inside of it). Then make it personal. Three things you love most about Mommy.

261. Get a library card and use it so vigorously that you wear down the numbers after just four months. Recklessly read books on topics you might otherwise ignore. If the book fails to spark your interest, return it and try another. If you fall in love with one, go purchase a new copy to keep in your own growing library. Read! Read! Read!

262. Find a recipe for the barbecue grill favorite, beer can chicken. The feast involves drinking half a can of beer and inserting the half-filled can inside the chicken so the can forms the base, with the chicken legs, of a sturdy tripod. The remaining beer moisturizes and flavors the food. It's a fun, odd, and delicious meal that takes about ninety minutes to cook, all of which can be spent drinking beer and marveling at the ingenuity of whoever dreamed up the delicacy.

263. In the garage or the kitchen, take used jars of baby food and screw the lids into the undersides of convenient shelves. It's a great space-saving way to keep handy stashes of paper clips, nails, screws, spices, etc.

264. Save the world through global "worming"! Take a vermiculture class from your local agricultural agent or recycling center. The practice involves feeding scraps of food—apple cores, potato and banana peels, tea

bags, etc.—to hungry red earthworms who convert the waste into nutrient-rich worm poo that makes excellent fertilizer for flower or vegetable gardens.

Colorful Days Diary

I'd planned on spending Earth Day scattering dense trash on pristine lands and in deep lakes where the environmental obscenities will likely linger for centuries.

Some future explorer would find them in some distant age. She may shake her head at my carelessness and exclaim, "Wow, someone with a really nasty slice used to roam these lands. We're miles from the nearest golf course!"

It is my Earth Day custom to bang Titleists deep in the Western Pennsylvania forests. I lose about four or five golf balls every single time I tee it up. I putt well, and my iron play is strong, but I can't hit a straight drive to save my life.

Most people don't consider lost golf balls trash. I do. I can't sleep the night before I golf, knowing there's nothing I can do to prevent defacing Mother Earth with my dimpled, nonbiodegradable spheres.

Maybe I take things too seriously.

Like saving the planet. I take it very seriously.

I aim to reduce, reuse, and recycle everything. I vowed last year I would never step over another piece of trash. Now I carry a recyclable plastic bag with me on my walks and usually have enough cups, wrappers, and papers to fill half a bag.

I could accumulate more if I wobbled along in a drunken sort of weave into the bushes and gutters, but that would take too long and would reduce the happy time I spend in the bar developing a true drunken weave the old-fashioned way.

Yet I know I could do more. I've read that the average American discards twenty-eight pounds of trash each week into our bulging landfills. Our family is way below that, but not near the average household in Oslo, Norway, where they produce just four pounds of weekly trash.

Four pounds! What, is Oslo populated entirely by Keebler elves?

Still, even they are pikers compared to the world's best recyclers. For every single pound of trash you and I produce, this trash-devouring little superhero is capable of recycling it into an equivalent amount of something useful and nutritious.

Behold, the red wiggler worm!

I did a story about the practice of vermiculture four years ago and immediately became enthralled with the ambi-sextrous red wiggler worms. The tiny slimies simply fascinate. It takes a trained eye and, I'd guess, an atomic-level microscope, but every worm is a hermaphrodite generously bestowed with organs of both sexes.

The condition is not enough to make me want to tune in to worm porn night on Animal Planet, but I'll never again look at another worm and believe it must endure a boring or lonely existence.

As it was explained to me, "These worms simply live to eat and reproduce. Basically, the worm is just a mouth, an anus, and a microscopic little brain."

I asked, given these base characteristics, how do red wiggler worms differ from the typical radio talk show host?

"Well, the worm actually contributes some good to society. About 45 percent of our entire waste stream comes from food and paper products, both of which are compostable materials. Worms can convert these common waste products into nutrient-rich soil fertilizer to energize your gardens."

I was sold. I got a little bin and a softball-sized ball of one thousand little wigglers, and soon our family started putting apple cores, banana peels, lettuce scraps, tea bags, potato peels, etc., into the bin along with showers of shredded newspapers. The warm worm poo makes great fertilizer.

So now when strangers ask what I do for a living, I always answer, "I'm a worm farmer."

And it's true. Sure, I do a lot of writing, but there's rarely even a penny of commerce involved in the exercise. I used to say blogging was the journalistic equivalent of running a lemonade stand until I realized that even eight-year-olds know enough to charge a quarter for a glass of lemonade.

Worm farming is a productive pursuit that reduces vile pollution. Some critics would argue that blogging is the exact opposite.

So instead of golfing on this Earth Day, I'm putting on my worm farmer bib overalls and am heading to Baggaley Elementary School in Latrobe, Pennsylvania, to teach my daughter's second-grade class about the joys of vermiculture or worm farming.

I've done it the past couple of years, and it's always a joy to see the kids fussing over the bin as the worms frolic amid all the rich poo.

But it's not all fun and games. I don't let the kids get too out of hand.

It might upset the worms.

And, take my word for it, no one wants to see a hermaphroditic red wiggler get all excited in front of a classroom full of second graders.

265. Argue vociferously that it's well past time for us to have flying cars. And it is! If enough people talk about it, soon someone's going to get the message. We want our flying cars!

266. Try not to confuse the words *irony* and *coincidence*, as too many people do. It's not ironic when two old friends of similar taste run into each other at the same B movie. It's coincidence. Irony is when a wolf eats a vegetarian.

267. No common "household" item has undergone greater and more fantastic advancements than the telephone. Try to imagine what far-fetched tech abilities the cell phone of the future will have. Write them down and see how your most fanciful guess was exceeded.

268. Remember to write a Father's Day card each year to Jack Somoano, the patron saint of Mr. Moms. When his wife delivered quintuplets in 2000, he agreed to stay home to raise the bawling sprawl while wife Kathy brought home the bacon.

269. Colorful conversation starter: Point out to fans of Southern Rock that since its founding in 1972, The Marshall Tucker Band has featured 27 different musicians and not one of them has been named either Marshall or Tucker.

270. It doesn't matter if you live in a desert hundreds of miles from the nearest body of water, stringing a hammock up between two strong cacti and jumping in lets you close your eyes and imagine you're at the beach. Every backyard or porch needs a Gilligan-worthy hammock. Be sure to use it for at least ten minutes every day the mercury peaks above seventy degrees.

271. Get a little countertop *"ding!"* bell, the kind used at hotel counters and roadside diner kitchen grills. Use it for meals when you need to summon the spouse and kids to help carry the food to the table. Try to sound a little gruff when you bark, "Order up!"

272. It only takes about ten days out of every two years, so revel in the Olympic competition. It always promises a great mix of quirky games and competitors who'll warm the heart of even the most jaded of sports fans.

273. Always fill out two NCAA pools during March Madness—a serious one in a big-money pool and a silly one against a child or some innocent who knows nothing about college basketball. Try to win the first and lose the second. You'll be surprised that neither effort will be as easy as it looks.

274. Marvel at the twists of history. Legend has it that when a visiting sea captain asked a native the name of a distant volcanic island in the Javan seas, a native boatman responded, *"Kaga tau."* The sea captain nodded and duly transcribed the response, "Krakatoa." Years later, anthropologists learned that *"Kaga tau"* means "I don't know."

275. Come up with your own six-word biography. Try to match one of the best, by humorist and author A. J. Jacobs, who summed up his entire existence thusly, "Born bald. Grew hair. Bald again."

276. Visit the national park in Shanksville, Pennsylvania, commemorating the heroes of Flight 93. It'll give you patriotic chills that'll endure forever. Then read Jere Longman's fine book, *Among the Heroes*, about the inspiring battle and the men and women who fought it.

277. Never fail to include in your cards to newlyweds heartfelt congratulations and this sage advice for a long and happy marriage: "Always argue naked!"

278. Urge expecting parents to bestow any male child with the best name in the history of baby boys: Buzz Sawyer. Think about it. Buzz hearkens to one of our greatest American heroes, astronaut Buzz Aldrin, and Sawyer reminds us of one our greatest literary touchstones, Tom Sawyer. Then sell it to the guys, saying the boy'll be destined for football greatness because so many announcers will be thrilled to yell the inevitable nickname "… and Buzz Saw Jones shreds another hole in the defense to score the Super Bowl winning touchdown!"

279. Never learn the sex of an impending birth in advance, and advise other expectant parents to avoid it. Hearing the doctor say, "It's a …" is one of life's last great surprises. It shouldn't be foregone just because someone's too impatient to wait on whether to paint the nursery pink or blue.

280. Always have a handy list of your three favorite Americans. It makes a great conversation starter and reveals as much about you as it does the United States. Always include at least one of the following: Ben Franklin, Mark Twain, or Bugs Bunny. Colorful people use all three.

281. Argue that one way to trim the staggering federal deficit is for the government to begin selling vanity zip codes. For instance, wanna bet Las Vegas wouldn't wager that the available zip code 77777 is worth at least $1 million in publicity?

Colorful Days Diary

For the sake of mental convenience, I'm thinking of packing up the family and all our stuff, and moving the whole shebang to Newton Falls, Ohio.

That way, I could age into eventual muddle-mindedness in the town that has perhaps the easiest zip code to remember in the entire United States.

Yep, welcome to Newton Falls, pop. 4,892, zip 44444. I don't think the town, about thirty minutes west of the dormant smokestacks of Youngstown, gets the acclaim it deserves.

I'm in the midst of a comprehensive study about zip codes for pinheads. It'll be two years ago in February that we moved one mile from near Latrobe, Pennsylvania, 15696, to postally proper Latrobe, Pennsylvania, 15650, and I still occasionally find my password-cluttered mind stumbling over the difference. It has me wishing I lived someplace where my zip had some zing.

Some place like, say, Schenectady, New York, 12345. Of course then I'd forever have to be spelling Schenectady, and that would never do.

We are a numerically obsessed nation that shells out precious dollars for vanity license plates, and we fret whenever the fickle phone company threatens to bump us from our familiar urban area codes to something less comforting.

For the good of the nation, it's time we extend that obsession to the humble zip code. I think it's time the government begins selling zip codes to communities that stand to profit from the panache.

Why, for instance, is Las Vegas 89123—a lousy fold 'em hand if ever there was one—when it could contribute $1 million to the national cause by paying for the unused 77777? Just think how much publicity it would get from the news if it paid for those lucky numbers, instead of having the ones randomly assigned by faceless bureaucrats at the USPS.

(Trivial Aside: the father of the zip code is a postal employee named Robert Moon, who submitted the proposal for a "Zone Improvement Plan" back in 1944.)

It's a sure moneymaker, and many cities and towns could have contests trying to claim one of the many unused numbers still available. And there are plenty of them. The post office only uses forty-three thousand out of the one hundred thousand possible five-digit combinations.

Many of the good and obvious ones are still gathering dust on the postal shelf. For instance, 44444 in Newton Falls is the only five-of-a-kind zipper in circulation.

According to my research, the lowest number in the system is Adjuntas, Puerto Rico, with 00601, which begs the questions: What happened to the first six hundred? Did someone think we'd someday annex Cuba and might need 00001 through 00600? The nosebleed award goes to Yukutat, Alaska, with 99689.

Bond, Colorado, appears to be perfectly insignificant to the rest of the world, but how much publicity could it gain if someone with a puckish sense of humor bestowed them the perfectly obvious 00007? Whenever a new Bond movie was released, reporters from all over the country would be descending on Bond to write reviews appearing under headlines like "Bond on Bond," or "License to Deliver, Bond 00007."

Same goes for Salem, Massachusetts, which labors under the clumsy postal designation 01970. Why not cash in on their witch-hunting history and brand the local post office with the mark of the postal beast, 00666?

My wife speculates stratospheric bidding between Houston and Cape Kennedy would launch over who most deserves the available countdown zip of 54321.

Brimfield, Massachusetts, looks like a line of binary code with 01010 and is among the lowest aggregate total of any zip code because the system includes no zip codes with four zeros and a single 1.

I could retire to Sunrise, Florida, with its full-house zip code of 33322. That'd be easy to remember.

(Trivial Aside No. 2: Sunrise is a planned retirement community that was originally named Sunset. But developers quickly found out that creaky retirees don't like being reminded that the sun is setting on their lives, so they nominally swapped the astronomical actions and sales grew robust. Sometimes perception is everything).

How much would Philadelphia pay to liberate 01776 from North Sudbury, Massachusetts? Philly is the birthplace of the greatest nation in the world. Having the zip code 01776 would be a constant mail reminder of that proud history. Why surrender it to North Sudbury, which gave the nation what? Geographic balance to South Sudbury?

For as long as I live, I'll never forget the phone number of a man who left a thriving dentistry practice to become a shepherd. I asked him the best way to get in touch for a story, and he told me, "Just dial GOD-BONE." That's what his number, 463-2663, spelled. I would think something similar could be done with zip codes.

New York could claim the unused 27753 (APPLE), coffee-mecca Seattle could splurge on BEANS (23267), and the beer makers in Milwaukee would doubtless bubble with enthusiasm at the opportunity to snatch SUDSY (78379) from Riviera, Texas.

(Trivial Aside No. 3: Trivial Aside would be a dandy name for my home blog if I ever get tired of EightDaysToAmish.com. In fact, it practically nails the sum accomplishments of what I've been doing my entire life.)

These kinds of trivial matters fascinate and distract me. Apparently, it is a code of enthusiasm I share with few others. I've pitched this idea to local postal officials for the past year or so. Would you like to know how much encouragement they've delivered to me?

You guessed it.

Zip.

282. Be a walking exclamation point, and people will be drawn to you. People shy away from people who walk around like question marks. Improving your posture will improve your friendships, and that's without question.

283. Purchase *The Art of Happiness: A Handbook for Living*, by the world's leading authority on happiness, the Dalai Lama. Read it while eating a big plate of cookies.

284. Describe the empty calories they sneak into manufactured foods as "garbohydrates" after the reclusive and unfulfilled actress Greta Garbo.

285. Discuss among friends the pros and cons of what will happen to the human race when parents are allowed to select the sex of their offspring. For instance, if more people choose boys, it'll be good for football but bad for peace.

286. After residing in it for several months, ask the people who just sold you their old home or apartment if they used to hide bags of money in odd places. If they say no and ask why, just smile and say, "No reason."

287. On a freezing winter day when record lows are predicted, include a box of popsicles in your frantic store purchases. Enjoy one and save the stick. Then eat lots of the tasty treats once summer arrives. Again, save all the sticks. Then the next freezing winter day, put on some Beach Boys music and use all the sticks to construct something that'll make you think of summer. Like a surfboard.

288. Celebrate without fail a lavish Christmas in July. As sacred and satisfying as the holiday can be, we all recognize it could benefit from some tyrannical improvements. Simply shopping for simple Christmas-in-July presents and decorations and wishing clerks a Merry Christmas in July will spread a welcome jolt of holiday cheer—six full months before the stress.

289. Point out that not all students need to be designated "gifted" to thrive as adults. Many successful adults spent their early years being shuffled between increasingly

indifferent educators. There's nothing wrong with growing up being, well, regifted.

290. In appreciation of one of our national treasures, take a weekend and listen in chronological order to every single song Bruce Springsteen's ever recorded. For four decades, he has chronicled the ups and downs of America and, in a way, much of your very own life.

291. Break bread with cynicism and understand what motivates the viewpoint. But save all the slow dances and most passionate kisses for optimistic emotions. Always.

292. Eat every part of the apple except for the sticklike stem. The rest is perfectly healthy, and consuming it represents a triumph over micro-waste. Plus, people will think you're earthy, and people like earthy people.

293. Once a year, take two big boxes of Lucky Charms and spend an hour or two separating the frosted toasted oats that nobody likes from the magically delicious marshmallows everybody craves. Surprise a kid with a bowl full of the sweetened charms. Be sure to have a bowl for yourself.

294. Tell the people you love that you love them. Say it aloud. And, yes, men, say it to other men.

Colorful Days Diary

I don't remember exactly when my brother and I started concluding nearly all our phone calls with "I love you," but it's become a natural declaration.

Because I do love him. Since the sandbox, he's always been a sort of hero to me. He's one of those great big brothers that never minded when I tagged along. I remember being the batboy for his sandlot championship baseball team.

When he left home to attend Ohio University, he shepherded me along on getaway weekends where I had the kind of fun that ensured I'd go there, too. It was one of the best things that's ever happened to me.

After I graduated from OU, I went to visit him in Nashville where he was working and I landed a job at the newspaper there. We became roommates. I'll never forget the two of us sitting on the little back porch drinking beers and watching the big jets glide in over Old Hickory Lake.

I think after our father died in 2004, we began to appreciate a special closeness, having been sons to a man so fun and rare.

None of that's really surprising. Sure, many siblings war throughout their lives and cause wicked tension at the family get-togethers, but the reverse is also true. Many enjoy the warm closeness that my brother and I have always felt.

What's unusual is that I'm beginning to feel strange urgings to tell other male friends that, yes, I love them, too.

Not in the way I love my brother, but I have many close male friends, three in particular, I love deeply, and I'm struggling with how to share this forbidden emotion.

Like most guys, I am emotionally repressed in how I deal with my dear male friends. I certainly feel a deep love for them, but I wrestle with how I should express those feelings.

I was thinking of this while I was listening to Kieran Kane's lovely rendition of the Louie Armstrong classic, "What a Wonderful World."

> *I see friends shaking hands, saying, "How do you do?"*
> *What they're really saying is, "I love you."*

Why is it so wrong for me to tell my male friends that I love them? Can't I, for the love of God, unshackle the societal constraints and convey what goes on in my heart to the men that matter most to me?

What would happen if instead of our standard buddy-buddy sign off—"Hey, man, you take it easy ... Go, Steelers!"—I took a different approach? What if instead of that breezy happy-hour send-off, I looked soulfully into Frank's cappuccino-colored eyes and said, "Frank, I love you ... Go, Steelers!"

I know exactly what would happen. Frank's bushy mustache would start to twitch the way it does when the bartender says he's shut off. Why, he'd be outraged. He doesn't want my love (even though I suspect he's always loved me, too). An awkward silence would descend on the bar. I'd be an instant pariah. Then all the cruel Brokeback Mountain jokes would start.

It's a strange fact of life in my still-redneck corner of the world that I could lose a friend because I dared to reveal how much he means to me.

It's not like I'm going to leave my wife and two kids for Frank. But guys like us are so emotionally remote that we have a difficult time acknowledging the genuine love we feel for—and this is even difficult to type—our "boy" friends.

Not anymore.

As of today, I'll no longer deny the urges that are becoming too momentous to ignore.

I'm going to freely expose myself to the risks that will come with saying without reserve, "Hey, I love you," to other men.

I'm going to start right here by telling the whole world of my earnest feelings for three darling buddies who've always touched me deepest in my soul.

Here goes ...

I love you, Moe!

I love you, Larry!

And I love you, Curly!

That wasn't as difficult as I thought it would be.

Nyuk, nyuk.

295. The most neglected surface in any structure or dwelling is the ceiling. It doesn't have to be, nor should it. Give the ceilings in basements or family rumpus rooms some life by dangling keepsakes from a fishing line.

296. Make a list of three movies you believe in watching at least once a year. Pull the list out on a rainy day, turn off the phones, lock the doors, and start making popcorn. Some suggestions: *Gone with the Wind, Shawshank Redemption, Jaws*—all timeless classics.

297. As you begin to age, scan the history books for a historic figure to whom you might bear a passing resemblance. Study him or her. Being a historic reenactor at schools or museums can be a fun and lucrative way to earn spare cash.

298. Try to do something that'll ensure you'll have a good day on April 14, a historically bad day. That's the day that Abraham Lincoln was shot, the Titanic hit an iceberg, and Greg Norman squandered a six-stroke back nine lead to blow the 1996 Masters.

299. "Dust bunnies" is a perfectly acceptable cutesy name for the collection of dust, hair, and fuzz tumbleweeding beneath your bed. But calling it "ghost poo" will seem more fun and original.

300. Next time you're stuck for a fun family vacation, think bourbon. No, this isn't a suggestion to get blasted to avoid family stress. In 2008, Frommer's picked the American Whiskey Trail, scattered primarily through charming hamlets in Kentucky and Tennessee, as one of the best family vacations in America.

301. Think about what your dream day in heaven will be like. Will you go to a beach with loved ones? Golf with your late grandfather? Meet historic heroes? Maybe dine with deities? Think and wonder how heavenly heaven will be. Then do something soulful to ensure you're going to get there.

302. If you can do so without hurting yourself, build a little tree house in your backyard. Do it for your kids. If you don't have kids, do it for yourself.

303. Always stay until the final credit rolls. It'll give you a chance to unwind while the traffic clears out and—who knows?—maybe spy the name of a distant relative working on some obscure job in the glamorous movie business. And sometimes colorful moviemakers reward their most patient viewers with funny surprises at the very end of the movie.

304. Be an idea person and come up with creative solutions to vexing problems. For instance, edible newspapers would eliminate waste and save the print news industry. The technology's been available since November 25, 2003, when a baked goods savant named Douglas Stewart was issued US patent #6,652,897. The patent means it's safe to consume certain papers and colored inks. Yes, Stewart's the genius who devised a way to print pictures and lacquer them atop birthday cakes. Think how it would help busy executives if they could read a page of the *Wall Street Journal* and eat it up like a salad. You don't have to go to the trouble of putting such fantastic ideas into practice. Remember, you're an idea person.

305. If you're going to go to the trouble of getting out of bed and getting dressed on a Sunday morning to attend church, be sure to pay attention and don't let your mind wander. Don't be one of those Bored Again Christians.

306. Say a small, fast prayer anytime you see a siren running on a speeding police car, fire truck, or ambulance. Chances are somebody's in trouble and somebody brave is going to help. And that's what prayer's all about.

307. Anytime you hear of someone dying suddenly, it should reinforce the need to ensure you're always living suddenly.

308. Don't be afraid to accept some parenting advice from pop stars like Elton John. He's right. Mars ain't the kind of place to raise your kids.

309. Next time you hear the government's imposed some sort of no-fly zone for security reasons, wonder aloud what kind of trouser fashion adjustments those in the area will need to make.

310. Tinker with daylight savings time to slow aging.

Colorful Days Diary

I love this turn-back-the-clock thing so much, I wish we could do it once a week. The cool thing about it is in twenty years, we'd only be about eighteen years older.

Yes, daylight savings time slows aging. But only by one hour.

If we did it once a week or maybe one minute per hour, we could live to be 175 years old.

I see many benefits. Gas prices would rise more slowly. Happy hour would be happy sixty-one minutes (and generous bar owners would feel obliged to round up). And the timeless game of baseball would seem endless.

Well, that baseball part would remain unchanged to those who fail to appreciate its nuance.

We've never used "time-out" as a disciplinary tactic. I guess it works for some, but it's too early to discern the long-term effects.

For instance, when this generation of misbehaving children grows up and starts attending college and professional sports, will they depart the arenas en masse and head for a quiet corner whenever a referee whistles time-out?

Again with baseball, it used to be popular for baseball franchises to have "Turn Back the Clock Day," when teams would dress in bygone uniforms and sell things like soda and popcorn for a buck and a quarter.

It was great fun, and we thought it would be wonderful if the whole city complied. So if you had a "Turn Back the Clock Day" to, say, 1929, beer citywide would be a nickel and commuters would have to find horses to ride to work.

I guess I'd like to turn back the clock to the 1950s when it seemed like it must have been a really great time to be a white male who liked to drink. That would have worked for me better than, say, if I were a black male who liked to vote.

So I'm pretty comfortable with our times. Despite all our many upheavals and the daily doom in the headlines, I'm optimistic about the future. I'm just not in that big of a hurry to have it come rushing up on us so quickly.

The exception, of course, being the year 2020 when my enduring insistence that 2020 will be a great year for visionaries is likely to finally gain marketing traction.

A friend of mine once said time is man's worst invention. That's very profound. As I'm becoming more conspiracy minded the older I get, I must conclude that the concept of time was conceived by the guy who'd invented the first clock but couldn't find a use for it.

So, voila, time! If you have one fussbucket with a timepiece, then everyone needs one.

I say to hell with time. Let's all just show up whenever we feel like it. And bring a book.

I have three watches I adore: one from my late grandfather, an Elvis one from my good buddy Quinn, and a really snazzy one generously gifted to me from a Las Vegas resort for work that didn't warrant the bauble. They gave one to my wife, too.

It was the oddest thing. We were there on an assignment for a now-defunct magazine. The magazines I've worked for that can now be described as now-defunct are too numerous to name.

But we were on a fancy lake cruise outside of town and our host presented us with two boxes from an elegant jeweler. Inside were these fabulous watches.

I said, no, we couldn't. It wouldn't be ethical.

As I was saying this, I was admiring the watch on my wrist and thinking, "It's a tad too snug, but I saw a jeweler in the casino. I'll bet he'll size it for free."

I was correct.

Ethical considerations be damned, there was no way I was leaving Las Vegas without that watch. It was magnificent.

To this day, my wife still thinks some husky guy is going to show up at our door and tell us we need to kill Vinny or he's taking back the watches.

I know this much: my wife will kill Vinny. She loves that watch. Me too.

But I'm thinking of making all three timepieces obsolete one of these days.

I'm thinking of getting a $75 tattoo of an $18,000 Rolex for my left wrist.

It'll be waterproof, impressive in refined company, and will make even the wafer-thin models look clunky by comparison.

I'll do it one of these days, I swear.

I just need to find the time.

311. Author Larry McMurtry remembers a time when his West Texas phone number was 9. Count on it: someday kids will marvel our numbers were just ten digits long.

312. Start a wager with your wife to see how long your young children will go before they start pronouncing "Mom" and "Dad" as two-syllable words.

313. No matter what the situation, how dignified or refined, always without fail, shout, *"Gesundheit!"* anytime you hear someone use the word "eschew."

314. Tell people you're nostalgic for the days when phones used to have busy signals—not because you're ever busy, but because it was nice having people you didn't want to talk to think you were.

315. Consider that the entire exercise of life might really be like those two or three hours we all have to kill while the hotel gets our room ready for the three o'clock check in.

316. You can learn lots about your exciting new love by finding out how he or she broke up with their last love.

317. Colorful conversation starter: ask people from Wyoming, our most geographically square state, how they ever manage to think outside the box.

318. Every Easter, try to enjoy at least one Cadbury egg, the delicious seasonal chocolate treat with cream filling. Then tell people if chickens ever start laying Cadbury eggs, you'll drop everything to become a chicken farmer.

319. Watch *The Wizard of Oz* every chance you get. There's not a wasted word, and the tunes are truly some of the catchiest in American history. Wonder to other viewers about the Wicked Witch of the West and how a single splash of water killed her. Logically conclude not only was she evil, but she also must have reeked.

320. Refer to teenage girls who starve themselves to appear more like popular Hollywood anorexics as "slimitators."

321. Ask right-handed people who do a lot of typing if they ever once use their left thumb in all the typing commotion. When it comes to typing, most people have left thumbs that never lift a finger.

322. Understand that a long marriage is a terrific antidote to excessive ego.

323. Remember to ask anyone who works in a crime lab if employees ever sit around singing, *"Someday my prints will come!"*

324. Be patient with your elderly parents. Encourage them. Be kind to them. Even when it seems their dying days will kill you, too.

325. Remind bloggers and prospective writers eager to achieve a larger readership that, with few exceptions, no one cares to read about your family unless Paris Hilton is in your family.

326. Describing the odd, tingly feeling you get below the ankle as having your foot "fall asleep" doesn't cut it for colorful people. Try saying you're suffering from "comatoes."

327. Warn with Biblical furor that society will descend into chaos in eighteen months whenever someone invents and begins marketing a credible lie detector app.

328. Parents stuck on long car rides listening to Radio Disney, unite! Urge your lawmakers to make it illegal for anyone to make music unless they're mature enough to have to shave something.

329. Call the dance you do every winter when you have to pat down thirteen different pockets to find one set of car keys, "The Arctic Macarena."

330. Always predict Super Bowl scores by using Roman numerals. Example: Detroit Lions XLVI, Buffalo Bills, XXVIII. It's annoying enough that perhaps it'll help speed the end of the pompous NFL madness of using the archaic practice to designate the big game.

331. Studies show it takes most people just thirty seconds to judge what kind of person you are. That sounds a little rushed. Try to give it about five years. These things take time.

332. Evil and devil have so much in common they should be pronounced the same: either it's E-vil and DE-vil or EV-il and DEV-il. Let's agree it should be EE-vil and DEE-vil. Sounds spookier.

333. Try to live your life with the understanding you'll never be lonely, bored, or broke as long as there are libraries and library cards. Then plan on having a convincing argument when your bank, the IRS, and your spouse beg to differ.

334. Understand that we're never going to solve world hunger until someone invents a machine that will allow anyone with leftovers a way to fax them still hot to the hungry. It'll happen. You watch.

335. Argue aloud with the news anytime they dismiss a distant earthquake as minor. Assure nearby listeners that every earthquake is in some way groundbreaking.

336. Take an exhilarating ride down a snowy hill on a five-person toboggan. Wonder if it would be possible to fit twenty-five people on a footboggan.

337. Follow the lists of most happy/least happy places to live and come to your own conclusions.

Colorful Days Diary

I experienced a momentary hiccup of dismay upon reading the list of least/most happy states. It said I'd spent nearly all of my most happy years in some of the most miserable states.

Understand, it didn't ruin my day. I learned years ago that I'm genetically disposed to happiness.

It's a sort of character defect along the lines of being cheap, lazy, or naturally unkempt (I'm three-for-three on those, too).

Yet, a foolish happiness is my most persistent trait. Been that way all my life. It's an unusual circumstance for anyone who bothers to read the newspaper, as I've always done.

Really, anyone who is at all aware of the news or earth trends should awaken borderline suicidal and become progressively more morose as the day progresses. There are mass bombings, random murders, thieves who prey on senior citizens, and here in Western Pennsylvania, we are besieged by the daily drumbeat of news that, gadzooks, the Steelers have been knocked from the playoffs.

How can anyone with an IQ above a hammer be happy?

The AP report I saw said the study was based on residential satisfaction with schools, safety, and commuting. By those criteria, Louisiana comes first in cheeriness.

Had more scholarly discrimination been applied, the study would have concluded that the top ten are blessed with an abundance of booze and beaches.

I wouldn't argue with Louisiana. I've been blissfully happy there many times. Once in New Orleans while there on a deep-pocket expense account, I was convinced I'd died and gone to happy heaven. It was wonderful.

In fact, if I ever get to actual heaven and someone doesn't say, "Welcome to New Orleans—here's the company credit card," I'm going to hunt around for a suggestion box.

I also have splendid memories of happy times in Florida, Tennessee, South Carolina, Mississippi, Alabama, and Maine, all states listed in the top ten.

If for some outlandish reason, someone told me I had to move back to Tennessee, I'd do it in a heartbeat. My big brother and his family live there, and I have many friends from the years 1985–88 when I called the Volunteer State home. I love the music at the Bluebird Cafe in Nashville, the barbecue at Rendezvous in Memphis, and all that fine bourbon produced in happy hamlets like Lynchburg and Tullahoma.

Heck, with enough Tennessee sippin' whiskey within reach, I could probably be happy in hell.

And I'd love to spend more time in the marvelous Lowcountry of South Carolina, as relaxed a location as anywhere in the nation.

But it looks like I'm doomed to spend my days here in Pennsylvania, now ranked the ninth least happy state in the union. As I tap out this post, I can look out the window and see snow falling that'll probably lie on the ground until late March.

I don't know why my fellow Pennsylvanians are so unhappy. Sure, our legislature is full of overpaid crooks, more than 10 percent can't even find work in the godforsaken coal mines, and the weather sucks from Halloween to clear past Easter.

Plus, if anyone ever made us sit in state-by-state homerooms, we'd be stuck with newly single Pennsylvanians Jon and Kate Gosselin.

But is it really all that bad?

Take me. I've hardly earned a dime all year and will stubbornly refuse wage-earning work if I think it's beneath me or cuts too deeply into my bar time. Yet I remain foolishly convinced today something good will happen to me whether I do something about it or not.

Here's a thought: maybe the only person they bothered to poll was my poor wife. Now, there's a person with ample reason to be unhappy.

Anyhoo, I was surprised that more of the geometrically boring states didn't crack the bottom ten. Kids are always being encouraged to "think outside the box." How is that even possible in a state as perfectly square as Wyoming (see tip no. 317)?

It's too bad we don't have one circular state. It's such a happy shape I'd love to live there in the round.

Square or round, I guess it wouldn't make any difference for a guy like me. I'm just stuck being happy.

I go through life like a retired fisherman with a fresh bucket full of worms and dirt, ever content to be whiling away the years with the patience and confidence that something good is bound to happen sooner or later.

I guess true happiness is just a state of mind where we can choose to reside or not.

338. Peppermint is one of the most delightful tastes to ever dance across the human tongue. Plus, it points out an

obvious opportunity for someone to invent a saltmint. That has the potential to be a wild and salty success.

339. Anytime someone says "the mind boggles" like it's some kind of rarity, point out that the majority of minds do more boggling than thinking.

340. Remember what J. R. Ewing, the sage of Southfork, said about the importance of ethics: "Once you get past ethics, the rest is easy." Then try to remember how many suspects police had when it came time to solve who shot J. R.

341. Whenever you hear someone poetically say that no two snowflakes are alike, offer him or her a snow shovel and opportunity to clear your driveway the next time it snows. It only takes about four minutes of shoveling to realize every single snowflake looks exactly alike when there are about a billion of them between you and a plowed road.

342. Try, on celebratory occasions, to deviate from the usual topics and offer a toast to toast, the world's best breakfast staple. Cheers to toast!

343. Tell people who are angry about bad weather forecasts that it's pointless when even drastic steps like storming The Weather Channel are clearly redundant.

344. Colorful conversation starter: ask friends if they know what they call female manatees. They call them manatees. Point out that manatees must be very chauvinist, and say it's surprising they don't make the gals all wear burkas.

345. Keep conversations lively by arguing we should change the national anthem to reflect the current moods of the

country and the president. Examples: Bill Clinton, "Don't Worry, Be Happy"; George W. Bush, "We Will Rock You!"; Barack Obama, "Why Can't We Be Friends?"

346. On the really boring days at work in the cubicle, take a few minutes to pretend you have a yah-yah job. That's one of those jobs where you sit on a pony and yell, "Yah! Yah!" at wandering livestock.

347. Confess to coworkers how you would enjoy being a heroic crime fighter with SuperVision, but you hate being a regular schlep with ordinary super vision. Explain the key differences.

348. Sir Isaac Newton is supposed to have been so brilliant he would wake up and sit on the side of the bed immobile, too paralyzed by genius to commit to further motion. His was one of history's greatest minds. Don't feel bad if you wake up and your first thought is, *Pop-Tarts or Lucky Charms?*

349. Send your Christmas cards to be mailed from Santa Claus, Indiana, 47579, the only town in America with a functioning United States Post Office named in honor of St. Nick.

350. On July 8 try and watch "The Poseidon Adventure," "Marty" "From Here to Eternity," or "McHale's Navy" to commemorate the life of the great Ernie Borgnine, who died on that day in 2012 at the age of 95. Realize Hollywood won't be the same until we find an Ernie Borgten.

351. Express your disinterest in doing something by colorful declarations. "That sounds as boring as mirror shopping with celebrities." Then change the subject by making tart observations about preening celebrities.

Colorful Days Diary

Brad Pitt is immersed in a fresh round of interviews complaining about how difficult it is being Brad Pitt.

This strikes me like carpenters complaining about nails or florists becoming disgruntled over the sight of yet another bloomin' rose.

I just don't get it. He makes movies and that may involve hidden tediums unseen by me, but essentially, movie producers pay him millions to be Brad Pitt. They want him to look dashing, be charming, and strike poses that make women swoon. If he's not up to it, then perhaps Pitt should quit being Pitt. Really, I can't imagine the acting side of it's all that tough.

In every grinding interview, he goes to great pains to assert how important it is to spend time with his enormous family, and I don't doubt him. Tribe time's important to me, too. But I have so few occupational burdens that our oldest daughter often gets exasperated enough to beg me to go out with my buddies so I don't intrude on her girly games with Mommy.

I pretend I'm wounded and grimly shuffle out the door like a repentant killer being dragged down death row for a court-ordered doom date with Ol' Sparky (see, Pitt's not the only one who can act).

He just released a well-received movie that clocks in at nearly three hours. I'm not familiar with movie production, but I can imagine filming took more than a few months away from Angelina, those eight or so kids, and the hypoallergenic squads of hand sanitizer-wielding nannies and other associated house help.

Maybe he should stop making movies. We could all do without him. There are hundreds of pretty young boys waiting tables in Hollywood who could, guaranteed, do what he does just as well without all the whining.

His biggest problem, it seems, are the paparazzi. He doesn't want people taking his picture. Or pictures of his family. Or his now-oppressive wife who just a few years ago was so outrageously exhibitionist she made Madonna seem shy.

But he knew when he was striving to be famous and when he chose to date and marry equally famous and whiny women that people would want to see pictures of him smiling, drinking excessively, and tripping on his way out of limousines. The rules haven't changed.

Him complaining about paparazzi is like me complaining about commas. I don't like commas. I wish we could get rid of them. I ruthlessly delete them every chance I get.

Sometimes I secretly try to play cat-and-mouse games with commas by using ridiculously long and structurally untenable run-on sentences that go on and on but in the end the winking little punctuation points usually assert themselves and bring order to grammatical chaos by doing their nimble if annoying little jobs, by golly.

I bring this all up because over the weekend my wife and I dropped the kids off with Grandma and enjoyed some sweetheart time. We considered Pitt's *The Curious Case of Benjamin Button*, but at three hours it was too much time away from the kids, so we chose Clint Eastwood and *Gran Torino*. It was outstanding. Go see it.

"That man can do no wrong," my wife said. "We're so lucky he's still around, still looking great, and still making these wonderful movies."

She's right. Eastwood's a bigger and more enduring star than Pitt could ever hope to be, but he's never complained about the burdens of being famous. He, like Robert Redford, Jack Nicholson, and the late and much-missed Paul Newman, gave us fantastic and relevant work that'll be enjoyed forever. And none of them ever made the job description "movie star" seem equivalent to ones like "bus driver" or "trash hauler."

On the contrary, they seem to enjoy it for the pleasure the rest of us suspect it must be. Eastwood's never been reclusive, hosts a PGA golf tournament, and once served as mayor of Carmel, California. Redford does important environmental work and unselfishly nurtures generations of aspiring filmmakers, and Newman's warmth and philanthropy were as monumental as his movies.

Nicholson? Well, his ebullient personal life is as audaciously entertaining as anything he's ever filmed, so no one cares that he's never devoted even a second to adopting underprivileged orphans or making charity salad dressings.

I remember a few years ago when Nicholson got into some petty open-container trouble for inviting paparazzi into the liquor store where he was hooch shopping and offering them a swig with a make-peace toast to the good life.

Maybe I should try that with commas.

352. You can be supportive of the whole sneeze-in-the-elbow movement and still wonder if it's been dreadful for people who enjoy square dancing.

353. Be in awe of professional broadcasters who can resist the urge to say "... with Israeli Prime Minister Benjamin NetanYA-HOOOO!"

354. Colorful conversation starter: tell people the dog that played Toto in *The Wizard of Oz* was, in fact, named Toto. Ask people if they think it was coincidence or just really expert casting.

355. Go ahead. When you're alone in a room with what is commonly described as a "magic marker," try to use it to change things like chairs into gold. You just never know.

356. If you have a cat or a kid, hang a feathered rattle or toy from the ceiling, just out of their reach. You'll catch yourself playing with it, too.

357. Consider how the words "time bomb" make no sense. It should be timed bomb. A time bomb might have its social advantages and could delay aging.

358. Realize that chefs with rashes are best at cooking from scratch.

359. Eating regular Oreos rather than Double Stuf Oreos is as pointless for people who want to be colorful as opting to watch movies featuring The Two Stooges.

360. You can be as green as the next person and still find something endearing about a fossil fuel that can be described as both "crude" and "refined." What range!

361. Fashions come and go, but no one colorful would ever argue on behalf of bringing back the old stovepipe hat. RIP, stovepipe hat.

362. Anytime you meet a dietician, ask if it would be possible to eliminate in one fell swoop both obesity and starvation if everyone, everywhere, would agree to eat just two meals a day.

363. Next time there's another spill along the lines of the Deepwater Horizon catastrophe of the summer of 2010, ask WWJCD—What would Jed Clampett do? Compared to the bumbling BP guys, the old oilman might have some homespun wisdom.

364. Colorful conversation starter: anytime you hear someone complaining about the morality of sex change operations, tell them that in the near future, sex changes will be common and the next moral question will involve whole species change operations. Yes, in the near future, unhappy humans will be able to become cats, parrots, etc.

365. Try and settle disputes the way artistic people do: they draw straws.

366. Avoid overuse of exclamation points!!!

367. Anytime you hear about all hell breaking loose in Greece, Africa, or the Middle East, think really hard about the last time you heard about all heaven breaking loose anyplace on earth and wonder why that never seems to happen.

368. Urge expectant parents to name any male offspring "Judas." Succeeding in life is largely a result of exceeding expectations, and people have historically set the bar pretty low for Judas.

Colorful Days Diary

Easter is the weekend I'm always chagrined we didn't have a son. By God, I'd have named him Judas.

One of the keys to succeeding in this life is simply to exceed expectations.

Being called Judas in the twenty-first century would ensure this. No name in history is freighted with worse connotations than Judas, and that would forever work in the kid's favor.

Fair-minded evaluators would say, "Naturally, I had my suspicions Judas was going to be a real turncoat, but I find him to be very trustworthy. I recommend we give him a raise. Let's start with thirty pieces of silver and see if he counters."

I'm always fascinated why some biblical names—Noah, Joshua, Samuel—endure, while others do not.

I've never met an Obadiah, a Nahum, or a Habakkuk, and that strikes me as strange. The world is awash with so many religious fanatics you'd think at least a few of them would honor the obscure Old Testament prophets rather than name yet another child Bob or Pete.

When Mr. and Mrs. Pilate named their son Pontius, they had no way of knowing they were passing along a handle that would terminate with his historic misdeeds. I feel for them. They must have been bursting with pride that their son had risen to be a powerful governor.

Here in America, we're always harping at politicians for doing what Pilate did: he slavishly followed the polls. Sometimes you just can't win.

With Pilate, they should have just term-limited the guy, not the name. Because when you think about it, Pontius is a great sounding name. It should be in play.

I think it would be fun for a family that was really into aviation to name a son Pontius and steer him into the airlines just so one day our routine flights from Pittsburgh to Charlotte could be enlivened by hearing the speaker crackle, "Hello, my name's Pontius and I'll be your pilot today …"

I've always loved the Elton John song, "Levon," and am stirred by the line, "He calls his child Jesus, 'cause he likes the name."

Levon's Jesus aspires to go to Venus on a balloon. I try to never let the senselessness of the lyric interfere with my enjoyment of a really great tune.

There have to be scores of men named Joseph who've married women named Mary, but I wager not a one of them had the playful audacity to name a son Jesus.

Too bad. A trio like that could start a dandy end-of-days cult, and that's where the real money is. Sex, too, from what I hear.

People of Spanish descent have no such sheepishness about naming males Jesus. They pronounce it as a joyful sounding "Hey! Zeus!"—which always sounds like an informal shout-out to a remote and powerful god with a human weakness for mortal women.

Kind of like Tiger Woods.

Major League Baseball is littered with Jesuses. The lowly Pittsburgh Pirates organization has a bunch of them, including Jesus Brito, whom we acquired from the Cleveland Indians.

And, get this—Jesus Brito was born in 1987 on December 25. I'm not kidding.

I don't care whether this Jesus can walk on water or not. I'll be happy if he can bat a measly .275 with runners in scoring position.

I like to think one day I'd be at the ballpark when some Jesus turns water into wine, but I know cheapskate owner Bob Nutting would spoil the miracle by charging $8.50 for a four-ounce plastic cup of the stuff.

Prior to the magical 2013 season, I had so little faith in the Pirates organization, my buddies and I used to joke that one day the Bucs would trade a guy named Jesus who'd been born on Christmas Day for two has-beens and a player to be named later.

But back to Judas. He's enjoying something of a renaissance. Biblical scholars are saying Judas was really Jesus's BFF and the only one the Nazarene could trust to fulfill scriptural destiny.

How they divined this, I have no idea. Maybe Judas had a Facebook page no one had ever bothered to check.

Of course, my name has a powerful biblical connection.

I am Christ-opher.

Before I'd bothered to look it up, I'd always assumed the "Christ" meant "Messiah" and "opher" meant "who toils in blogger obscurity," and I was only living up to half the bargain.

In actuality, it means "one who bears Christ in his heart."

That pleases me.

Still, I think I'd have done better if I were associated with the worst name in the Bible, rather than the best.

And, hell, it's been ages since anyone's offered me a cash equivalent of thirty pieces of silver to do anything.

369. Understand that molar, bicuspid, and uvula are all words of mouth.

370. Try to find a sound reason why the Gulf of Mexico isn't logically and simply called the Mexican Gulf. Instead, don't try. It's impossible.

371. Eat organic and green whenever possible, or realize that soon, eating from any end of the food chain is going to take actual teeth of steel.

372. Relax. It's perfectly normal to start thinking about the kids going back to school before they're even out for the summer. It doesn't make you a bad parent, and someday they'll understand.

373. Ask friends how champion water skiers ever practice. Aren't dry runs for them impossible?

374. Don't feel the least bit silly about praying for simple things. He's heard it all before, and reputable clergy assure us God doesn't use spam filters.

375. Recall whenever he's mentioned that George Orwell (1903–1950) had a little sister. Point out it's possible

she complained every once in a while ol' George was a tyrannical big brother.

376. Foolish mortal! You think you can tell time. Remember, time tells you!

377. Colorful people can be llama farmers, but only if they agree to never call any of their llamas Dolly.

378. If you ever do something that leads network cable shows to ask reality-show train wrecks like Danny Bonaduce about mistakes you're making in public, take that as a sign you've become too colorful.

379. For the sake of spiteful accuracy, refer to the artist Prince as "The Artist Formerly Known as The Artist Formerly Known as Prince."

380. Always be open to romance, even when you're tired. People who fake sleep to get out of lovin' are bulldozers.

381. Call one of the obscure cable shows and pitch them an idea for an antiquing show that would feature former *Happy Days* star Erin Moran seeking quirky items at offbeat shops around the country. Suggest they call it *Joanie Loves Tchotchke!*

382. Anytime you see cured ham on a menu, tell the waiter or waitress you'd like some ham that's never been sick. Say you'll only take ham that's never needed curing.

383. Try to think of a way to promote an all-important National No-Hype Week that wouldn't trample on the importance of the message.

384. Argue with poetry lovers that in terms of raw impact, succinctness, and message mission, history's greatest

poem may be "Be kind, Rewind." Even Shakespeare can't touch it. Explain it to kids of the digital age.

385. Strive to do things that will earn you a proverbial feather in your cap, but try to at all costs avoid wearing caps with feathers.

386. Always make a big deal of it anytime anyone offers you horseradish. Gush on and on about the remarkable equine that can garden as well as do all the other fun horsey stuff.

387. Never make the mistake of sipping life. Sip wine. Gulp life.

388. Refer to religious reporters stationed in the Vatican assigned to full papal coverage as "poperazzi."

389. Until there is a Jesus of Toledo, it is religiously redundant to refer to Him as Jesus of Nazareth. In religious conversation, just say Jesus. We'll all understand about Whom you're talking.

390. Colorful conversation starter: ask people if they think all the other kids made fun of him because Jeremiah was a bullfrog.

391. Urge Major League Baseball fans to get behind the idea of starting a MLB Steroid User Hall of Fame. Suggest the hall have injection ceremonies instead of induction ceremonies, lab coats instead of blazers, etc.

392. Refer to people who are adamant that we can still use all the fossil fuels we want as global warming SCOPEtics— people who think no matter the pollution, things will still turn out all green and minty fresh.

393.   Be moderate in all things, and that includes moderation. The philosophical distinction will allow you to be joyfully excessive whenever you feel like it.

Colorful Days Diary

I don't know how the conversation about milk got started, but it sounded like it was being conducted in a cafeteria full of fourth graders.

"I hate milk!"

"Eww! My mommy made me drink it all the time. Never again!"

But these weren't nine-year-olds. We were old men in an old man's bar.

Rather than little toddler cartons of milk, we were imbibing Scotch, bourbon, gin, rum, and beer! Beer! Beer!

We weren't drinking these spirits to strengthen our bones. We were drinking spirits to lift our own.

"Beer is proof that God loves us and wants us to be happy," is what sudsy sage Benjamin Franklin is said to have opined.

You can agree with that philosophical nugget and still be surprised, as I was, to hear my fellow inebriates expressing such visceral disdain for milk.

They talked about it the way they talk about the Taliban.

They want to see it banished from the face of the earth.

To me it was like hating Girl Scouts.

Milk is the ivory issue of the breast—and I know these guys love breasts. We watch cooking shows most every afternoon and, guaranteed, it isn't so we can learn how to expertly poach zucchini. Believe me, values voters wouldn't want to know what's going on in the minds of some of these guys when Giada de Laurentiis starts pounding her chicken.

And please don't mistake that example for deviant behavior. Culinary chicken pounding happens all the time in even Presbyterian kitchens.

Me, I love milk. True, I adore bourbon, tequila, vodka, oaky cabernets, and buttery chardonnays—you name it.

Many years ago, I had an unfortunate encounter with Southern Comfort, and we've never made peace. But I don't hate it. I simply try to avoid it because I know it's likely to make me vomit.

Sort of like Cubs fans.

But there are many times when a big frosty glass of milk really hits the spot. I often have it over Lucky Charms and with other breakfast staples.

This might strike some as odd, but I love milk with pasta. I've had many spaghetti meals that involved beer, milk, and water.

I admit it must have been awkward when the three of them got together in my stomach. It would be like a Jew, a Muslim, and that Koran-burning Florida whack job getting stuck in the same elevator.

There are many studies that say milk is essential for strong bone growth.

Not surprisingly, these studies are funded and promoted by— ta-da!—our nation's dairy interests!

I do know one person who is never going to expire from a milk deficiency.

That would be my wife.

She's admirably conscientious about her health and that of those around her.

But our oldest daughter absolutely detests milk, and it drives my wife crazy. I fear our efforts to infuse her with the daily recommended amount of calcium will backfire and that one day she'll be like the guy three stools down.

"Yeah," he said, "my mom used to make me drink it every day. I couldn't stand it. Just hated it. I haven't had a single glass of milk in the twenty-seven years since I left home. Won't even have it my house."

In maybe only this one regard, this flabby soon-to-be candidate for a liver transplant is exactly like one of the most fanatically fit men in history.

He's the late Jack LaLanne.

I interviewed him for a *Men's Health* story about six years ago.

He turned ninety-six in 2010. I expect he did remarkable things right up until his death the next year.

When he turned seventy in 1984, he fought strong winds and currents to swim 1.5 miles across Long Beach Harbor. He did it while handcuffed and shackled.

It gets better.

He did it while towing seventy boats with seventy people on board.

Talking with him was one of the most amazing and euphoric conversations I've ever had. The man's a marvel.

It was so amazing, I said to him, "Hey, my wife's right here. Will you mind telling her something inspirational?"

No problem.

They talked for ten minutes. Then my wife set the phone down, drove straight to Pittsburgh, dove into the Allegheny River, and towed with her teeth a coal barge fifteen miles upriver to New Kensington.

God bless him, the man's that positive and uplifting.

In fact, I can only recall one negative comment.

And it was about milk.

"French people live the longest, and they have wine with lunch and dinner every day. Americans drink milk instead. Milk is for a suckling calf. How many creatures still use milk after they're weaned? Just one. Man. I'd rather see people drink a glass of wine than a glass of milk any time of the day."

So if the world's most fit man hated milk, there's only one thing to do.

Wine for breakfast!

Any fitness advice that involves increasing our convivial alcohol consumption is something that simply must be milked.

394. Next time you hear a reporter cite a police source, swear you heard the reporter say a "police horse," and then hang in there and hope it's a talking pony.

395. Certainly we can all agree that angels have wings. But do they have gills? If, God willing, I become an angel, I hope I can enjoy some gearless scuba time. That would be cool.

396. Life is hard and riven with pain. Remember to dance anytime you hear music.

397. Argue that if coral is a stony ocean rock and corral is a pony pen, then corrral should be an oceanic enclosure to keep seahorses.

398. Find an expectant couple named the Shaws. Urge them to name any male offspring Rick because a man named Rick Shaw is bound to have a great future in the ground transportation business.

399. Open an art gallery with nothing on the walls. Then invite people to enter and be greeted by forty guys who say nothing but, "Hi, I'm Art."

400. Become an amateur acupuncturist any time you're feeling stressed. Firmly press two fingers on the acupressure point right under the middle of your collarbone and breathe deeply. Professional acupuncturists say it disperses tension.

401. Surreptitiously slip notes into the pockets of pants at clothing stores claiming to be from a slave laborer who earned a quarter during the day the pants were made.

402. Don't run power tools for more than an hour. Overuse and too many difficult projects without a reasonable break will wear out your power tool, eventually rendering it useless. Remember, the same can happen to you, too. Be sure to give yourself a break.

403. Try to think of what Elmer Fudd does whenever he sees Bugs Bunny grabbing a bigger musket the next time you're on Twitter and see the word "Retweet!"

404. If you see someone rushing through a subway or driving like a jerk, give the person the benefit of the doubt and stand aside. Who knows? Maybe you've just seen a doctor rushing to the hospital to deliver triplets.

405. Put down the smartphone in elevators and engage in the old-fashioned act of small talk. It's social networking unplugged.

406. Eat at least one ounce of dark chocolate each and every day. Nutritionists are calling it the new superfood. Do it while you can because, guaranteed, someday they'll turn on the treat and find something bad to say about dark chocolate.

407. Put the words "Do one really good deed" on a weekly to-do list and then make it a mission. You'll find someone who needs help and will be surprised by how much better you'll both feel.

Colorful Days Diary

It was more a wish than a prayer, more an expression of dissatisfaction that I was unable to have more of an impact on humanity.

I thought, *Gee, I wish I was in position to do more good deeds.*

That's the kind of thinking I do on my daily strolls around the neighborhood.

I'm not talking about saving cats from trees or diving in front of a bullet intended for an unworthy target. I don't have an urge to don a cape and save the world. It sounds like too much work.

But I thought it would be nice to help some little old lady across the street so she'll know the world isn't as scary as the headlines all hint.

Lo and behold, not a half mile into my walk, the opportunity to do a true good deed nearly fell in my lap.

It wasn't a little old lady. It was a big middle-aged one.

My description will sound contrived, but I swear it is factual.

She was what Dr. Hannibal Lecter described as "roomy." That was his euphemism for a woman of large proportions. She had stringy hair, was sweating profusely, and as I was about to discover, she had no front teeth.

It may be unkind, but my first impression was that from behind she resembled a pack mule, an observation based on her appearance and her apparent mission. She was carrying six plastic bags strained full with groceries—three bags in each hand—and a surfboard-sized raft of generic toilet paper.

She and I were both walking in the same direction on this humid, eighty-five degree day. I was gaining on her fast. She sat down one armload of bags to adjust and catch her breath.

Now, understand, I didn't specify in my wish that the recipient of my good deed resemble a movie star.

That didn't enter my thoughts. So if this was a test, I passed with flying colors.

"You look like you could use a hand," I said.

She smiled, a little embarrassed, that toothless smile scary enough to make an orange jack-o'-lantern green with envy.

"Oh, no, I'm fine," she said.

"Nonsense," said I. "Please let me assist."

It didn't take too much convincing for Donna to agree. I told her I was out for a walk and was happy to help. With sweat drops rolling down both of our noses, we proceeded.

She had about a mile to go, she said. No, she didn't own a car. She walked about once every two weeks to the grocery store and lugged it all back to her Main Street home.

She was very pleasant and grateful, but I was struck by how much awkward silence is involved in a mile-long walk with a perfect stranger.

She'd certainly seen enough TV to know that lots of no-good trouble can come from walking home with a stranger. And, me, I've read enough *Penthouse Forum* letters to know that interesting things can happen when meeting a stranger.

She may have wondered if I was a psychopath (I'm not—at least, not yet). She may have wondered if I was going to ask for money or sex. I wondered if she was going to offer me sex.

It wasn't easy work and may have been worth a little sex. The four bags I was toting seemed to weigh twenty pounds each.

"You're making me carry the heavy ones, aren't you?" I joked.

If she was nervous about me, she gave no hint of it. She smiled pleasantly almost the whole way. I think she was really grateful I came along when I did.

I was glad, too. I wonder if Donna would have gotten into my car if I'd have pulled over to offer her a ride.

Probably not. I doubt I would.

During one of our block-long silences, I started hoping my friends and people from church would drive by and recognize me.

The sight of me walking and carrying the groceries of a strange, large woman armed with enough toilet paper to weather a nuclear winter would have made for a dandy scandal, one I'd have been happy to nurture.

We did look like a couple, I'm sure. She was smiling because someone had stopped by to ease her burden on a miserable day.

I was smiling because my spontaneous urge to do a good deed had been fulfilled. It gave me a soulful sort of happiness to have by chance been in a position to help someone who really needed it.

I got to her door, set the groceries down, and said I was glad to have been able to help and enjoyed meeting her.

She smiled a big old toothless grin and spared us both any additional awkwardness by just saying thanks rather than inviting me in for a topless massage.

I felt so good on the long walk home I decided that tomorrow I'd start my walk by wishing my activity would include the discovery of a million dollars.

I'll let you know if that works out as well as this did.

408. Use the word *humbug* year-round and understand that it has nothing to do with Christmas. It's a great word Charles Dickens stole for Christmas, and we need to steal it back. Humbug has more to do with Vegas magicians and reality TV than it ever did with Christmas. In fact, you can hear the Scarecrow insulting the Wizard of Oz as a dastardly "Humbug!" after he's been exposed as

fraudulent. If even people with straw-stuffed brains can get it right, then so can the rest of us.

409. Practice "bizospice" care (pronounced biz-OS-pice care like HOSpice care). That means find a struggling local business and stay with them until the business either closes or revives and comes back to life. Either way, the struggling owner will be buoyed by your support.

410. Be sure to do something mean-spirited and incompetent every September 29, birthday of the late Larry Linville. He was the five-time married actor who played the indelible moron Major Frank Burns on M*A*S*H. Tell people you're doing it as a goof to honor Frank Burns, and they'll think you're colorful. Do it without telling them, and they'll just think you're a jerk.

411. Write facts about your birth that will ensure children consider you colorful. For instance, all the textbooks in North Korea say that on the February 16, 1941, birth of late despot Kim Jong-il, spring suddenly bloomed and the country was showered with a spontaneous outbreak of rainbows like those that happen in all the Care Bear stories. But do it to be colorful, not because you want to be like the cruel and tyrannical North Korean despot.

412. Treat your body like it's a cherished employee and you're striving for boss of the year stature. Encourage it to sleep in. Listen to its complaints. Discourage it from stressful activity. Pamper it. Be sure to treat your significant other the same way every once in a while.

413. Never multitask. Devote all your attention to whatever you're doing before moving on. If you're watching TV, don't let the computer distract you. If your child asks you a question, offer your full attention. Refuse to walk and chew gum at the same time.

414. Let people know of your priorities by signing off Tuesday's e-mails with things like, "And have a really great weekend!" even though you haven't even reached over-the-hump day.

415. Try to find an ark that didn't belong to Noah. It seems like in the entire recorded history of man there's only been one ark and it was Noah's. No one's ever heard of Mel's Ark or Burt's Used Arks.

416. Next time in New York, try to visit the Aphrodisia Herb Shoppe at 264 Bleecker Street. The exotic shop has nearly every herb known to man, and they'll be happy to mix essential oils that will cure your sour moods and enhance your good ones. Studies show the pleasures of scent recognition are beyond dispute.

417. Float down a lazy river on an inner tube.

418. Always take advantage of the gift-card note offer in most mail-order purchases. It's fun to order something from, say, a Bob Dylan website and have them compose a note to you that makes it sound like Dylan knows who you are and is grateful for your support. Lay it on thick. Show it to friends.

419. Make sure to always joyfully sing in church so that no one will ever confuse hymns with hums.

420. Prejudge nothing. Not even things unfairly called "stinkbugs."

Colorful Days Diary

I can't help but think that right now some stinkbug dad is telling his stinkbug daughter she is beautiful and can grow up to be anything she wants to be. And it breaks my heart to know the stinkbug daughter is wailing in despair, "But, Dad, I'm a stinkbug, and a stinkbug is all I'll ever be!"

It saddens me whenever the world imposes preconceived notions on any of God's creatures simply for the way they were born.

I'm so liberal even stinkbug bias offends me.

Man, do stinkbugs have it tough.

Talk about having the deck stacked against you. Being called "stinky" is one of the worst things that can happen to a kid. How would you like it if your entire race was referred to with that cruel pejorative?

Even third-world leaders would be loath to welcome the stinkbug president into their offices for a friendly meet 'n' greet.

I can only guess stinkbugs were created so that even the lowly dung beetle can sometimes feel a necessary surge of self-esteem to help it endure its universally grim thirty-six-month lifespan spent rolling balls of dung across arid cow pastures.

Dung Beetle: "Oh, woe is me! I spend my entire day balling nutrient-rich dung to feed a family whose breath is so foul we never dare kiss or show affection. Oh, well. Least I ain't no damn stinkbug!"

I think most of the world's wars were started by people who were determined to compensate for some slight that led to low self-esteem.

I vow that's not going to happen with my precious loved ones. Not on my watch.

I may be failing at providing much in the way of material goods for my two daughters, ages ten and four, but, by God, these girls will know they are loved, they will know they are smart, and they will know they are beautiful.

They will know all this because their daddy made it a point to tell them so each and every day.

My fear is at some point they will one day read this and know their daddy is an idiot because he spent a lot of time writing about things like the feelings of stinkbugs instead of seeking a paycheck.

I've seen scores of people on the news complaining bitterly about stinkbug infestations. Some say that when squashed they emit a skunk-like smell. Others compare the odor to that of rancid old sneakers.

It's a smell I cannot describe because I've never squashed a single stinkbug and I never will.

Unlike so many of my discriminating brethren, I'm perfectly at peace with the stinkbug.

In fact, I admire that, unlike bloodsucking bedbugs, the stinkbug does nothing untoward to humans until we extinguish them. Then, like a foul soul ascending to stinkbug heaven, the smell begins to rise.

To avoid that eventuality, experts advise homeowners to seize the stinkbug and flush it down the toilet—a not unreasonable place to dispose of something that begins with stink.

Me, I cradle them in a tissue, march them to the back porch, and give them a little pep talk.

"I have no quarrel with you, stinkbug, so I'm setting you free. I wish you health, happiness, and a competent press agent who'll help you overcome the stigma of your off-putting name. Now, go and be free! And if you come back, better not let the missus catch you or else she'll flush you right down the crapper."

I don't know whether my little speech is heeded or is met with deaf ears. Heck, I don't even know if stinkbugs have ears. Despite my heartfelt promotions, all I really know about stinkbugs is it's unwise to squash 'em.

But I believe every stinkbug should have the opportunity to overcome hateful perceptions.

I hope one day teams of entomologists will reveal that a rare stinkbug has been witnessed transforming itself into the most beautiful butterfly ever seen.

Dedicated entomologists would no doubt be bug-eyed at the sight, but that would, of course, be redundant.

How can dedicated entomologists be anything but bug-eyed?

But I will not rest until we banish all bias from man, animal, and insect.

That kind of obnoxious behavior really bugs me.

I think it stinks.

421. Refer to children who get drowsy after an afternoon of frenzied playground activity as "park splugs."

422. Euphoria is a state often observed in other people who are joyfully happy. Make sure you find time to engage in a little mephoria.

423. Be positive and associate yellow with sunny, not surrender. And paint the walls yellow in at least one room to remind you of sunshine on even the dreary days of winter.

424. All hail toothpaste! The only poison we all put in our mouths. Each tube of toothpaste contains enough poison to kill a small deer, and it hints at this on the warning labels. Yet it does no harm. In a world riddled with so much toxic violence, it's nice to know there's at least one poison so pleasant that every day it does something dazzling to brighten all our smiles.

425. Have the four-year-olds crank call grandma pretending to be the president.

426. Play "She's Gone," the 1987 song by Daryl Hall and John Oates, with the volume turned up to full. It's taken some of us more than two decades to realize it, but the song is one of the most finely crafted pop ditties ever recorded.

427. Never sit at work in the same position for more than thirty minutes. Experts say our bodies are meant to be in motion. Feel free to ignore this manic fitness chestnut anytime you feel like getting up and walking away from work to see a long, soul-soothing matinee.

428. Advise children that being cool isn't cool. Then do everything you can to keep your cool alive for as long as

you can. Being cool and doing cool things is one of the most important items on any adult's spiritual resume.

429. Help save the planet. Let the grass grow. One of man's most confounding habits is the drive to keep a lawn trimmed. If everyone weren't so picky, we could save a fortune on fuel.

430. Colorful conversation starter: point out to doomsayers that Armageddon isn't necessarily the worst thing that could ever happen. Anatomically speaking, Armageddon would get its buttocks kicked by Legmageddon.

431. Be a Johnny Nappleseed. Tell friends about studies that show power nappers experience benefits in both the mind and body, and it worked for renowned nappers like Albert Einstein, Winston Churchill, and Leonardo da Vinci.

432. Open a beauty salon and call it "Hip! Hip! Hair-ay!"

433. Don't let a near-death experience ever get in the way of a really good time.

Colorful Days Diary

I can say without hyperbole I nearly died yesterday.

I lead a soft life bereft of danger. My health is good and exposure to threats minimal.

That meant Sunday in New York elevated all my risks. I'd be inebriated in an unfamiliar city, increasing the chances I'd stumble in front of a speeding taxi or get gunned down by any of the numerous homicidal maniacs who call the Big Apple home.

Any of that would have at least made an interesting death story, and I'm all for that.

That's why my near-death experience would have been fatally embarrassing to my humble legacy, had I not survived it.

Blame it on a bacon-armored shrimp.

John and I were enjoying dim sum at the Golden Unicorn Restaurant in Chinatown. Dim sum is a great exotic treat where the food is served on little carts pushed by waitresses offering trays of tiny feasts. The girls bring the carts past, and you point with your chopsticks at what you want.

It's wonderful.

And John, my most corrupt and soulless friend, is great company. He's witty, profane, and so sacrilegious I imagine dining with him would be much like sharing dim sum with Satan.

Our bellies were full from an hour of rapacious overeating. Yet, we pressed on.

I don't remember how it happened. I may have been distracted by my eagerness to work the words "dimolition derby" into the conversation whenever the carts collided, but the blame mainly goes to simple poor manners and rampant gluttony.

I didn't even realize I was choking.

All I remember was my body started shutting down. I reached for a glass of water, and my hand started to shake violently.

I don't remember feeling pain. Only bewildered alarm.

I remember ordering my body to behave. I didn't want to make a scene, even as I was choking to death.

An unchewed golf ball–sized chunk of lightly fried shrimp wrapped in crunchy bacon was lodged in my throat.

Now, I know better than that. But as this was a Chinese restaurant, the custom is to use chopsticks, the most ridiculous dining utensil ever conceived to convey food from table to mouth.

You can't saw steak with chopsticks. It takes practice to skillfully pick up some General Tso's chicken, let alone a slippery pork dumpling. They are inferior to even the spork, a really handy innovation that by all logic should reduce by a full third the space of every single silverware drawer in the world.

But after an hour of using the chopsticks, I'd gotten careless. I didn't want to bite the piece in half and risk having the remainder plummet into a puddle of soy and splash unsightly stains on my shirt.

So I just shoveled the whole chunk into my mouth.

John later said it lasted about a minute. He thought I was having a seizure.

Somehow, I got that sucker down through pure will alone. I restored to normal almost immediately, and we began to piece together what had happened.

The incident, of course, dominated the conversation the rest of the day. I didn't see my life pass before my eyes or enjoy a cosmic conversion, and I took away no great lessons other than the reinforcement of the ones my mother told me about proper table manners.

I haven't vowed to lead a better life, cast off any unsavory habits, or enjoy this precious life any more than I already dearly do.

We spent the rest of the day just as we'd planned. We hit the bars and whooped it up with unbridled revelry.

John, of course, is already spinning the story to his advantage. He said today he intends to compose an e-mail telling all our friends about my piggish behavior and the heroic steps he took to save my life, a complete fabrication that I fear will somehow take hold in spite of the lies.

I don't think it's any exaggeration to say I could have died right there. People choke to death all the time. And that's not the way I want to go.

I have no fear of death as long as it doesn't have to hurt. I argue the best way to go is to die peacefully in your sleep of multiple gunshot wounds, which isn't nearly as contradictory as it sounds.

I can now say there isn't much real pain involved in nearly choking to death. The body just seems to check out. I'm happy I'll soon be home in the arms of my loved ones who, despite all my jokes, need me around for many more productive decades.

John selfishly wondered what would have happened to him if I'd have died. Would he have been stuck with the whole bill? Could he have persuaded the manager to offer him and a guest a free meal to compensate for the unpleasantness he'd endured the day his old buddy died?

I asked John to describe how I looked as the death mask tried to descend on my face.

"Oh, it was awful," he said. "Your face was turning bright red. Your eyes were bulging, and you were shaking like you were going to overturn the table. I thought you were a goner. It was very disturbing."

I told him I was surprised by his humanity.

"Oh, I didn't mean I was disturbed for you. I meant it was disturbing for any of us who had to see it."

So I'm damn glad to be alive today. Every day, really. I hope you are, too.

And I hope when I do die, it will be quick, tidy, and far from my evil friend who's disappointed he couldn't use my untimely demise as a bargaining chip for a free meal.

434. Remember, it's not a left lane. It's a passing lane. Apply your turn signal, get over, pass, and get back.

435. Don't let anyone you really care about get married until they're about thirty-five. Willie Nelson says there are no such things as ex-wives. There are only additional wives. Always respect the wisdoms of Willie.

436. Think about Albert Einstein whenever you think about the meaning of life. A nineteen-year-old college student asked Einstein about it, and here's what the genius said. "The answer is, in my opinion: satisfaction of the desires and needs of all, as far as this can be achieved, and achievement of harmony and beauty in the human relationships." In short, he said we're here to help each other ... and encourage people to stay the heck out of the passing lane.

437. Tell people the only time bitch, bitch, bitch ever turns into something positive is when you're running a robust dog-grooming business.

438. When faced with an unpleasant home improvement project, insist on your right to shout profanity and order the wife and kids out of the house for the weekend. Then have your buddies over for a pizza and beer party to help with the work.

439. Ask opticians if they're hopeful the year 2020 will be a great time for visionaries.

440. Buy a season's worth of your favorite cans of soup and capriciously remove all the labels when you get home.

441. Tell the waitresses and bartenders to hold the straws. Always. Straws are among the world's most useless instruments and a source of tremendous waste. Be like James Bond, who famously asked that his drinks be shaken, not stirred. James Bond doesn't suck, and neither should you.

442. Ask guys named Gord if anyone ever calls them "Punkin."

443. Try to imagine how much better off we'd all be if the humble micro-economic principle, "Need a penny/Take a penny/ Have a penny/Leave a penny," were applied on a global level.

444. Play *The Price Is Right* with in-home repair estimates. Make the contractor, plumber, or electrician play the Drew Carey host role.

445. Never let a child grow up being a total nomad; that is, don't let a youngster get away with shouting "No!" to every question or being mad all the time. Try to encourage all the children to be yes-happy.

446. Point out that if brevity truly is the soul of wit then obviously it should be "Brevity hearts wit."

447. Pretend with old friends that you still remember the phone number of your favorite pizza joint back in college. There'll be no way to check, and they'll be impressed by your trivial recollection.

448. Have the kids watch a celebrity interview program with you and then let them interview you about how you met their mom, what you dreamed about being when you grew up, and if you were ever cool.

449. Chefs get bored, too. Enliven your meal and your chef's day by requesting you be surprised with something that isn't on the menu.

450. It's a fact no one will broadcast: the more time you spend hearing other people broadcasting their own opinions, the less time you have to draw your own. Colorful people think for themselves.

451. Try to go to bed hungry at least one night a week. The endeavor will certainly help your efforts to control your weight, and the simple exercise will bestow you with a profound compassion for those who involuntarily do it every single night of their lives.

452. When making appointments with doctors, always choose the first appointment after the lunch hour before their schedules have a chance to get way out of whack.

453. If you're ever staying at a nice hotel, say you've lost something snazzy—maybe gloves, a scarf, etc.—and see if they'll let you plunder the lost and found.

454. On the most miserable morning of the year, set the alarm for thirty minutes earlier than usual. Then pull on the boots, the scarf, and the frost-fighting gloves and head over to the neighbors' driveway with your windshield snow scraper. Clean all the snow off the vehicle and then vamoose before they know who did it.

455. Each time you change the batteries in the smoke alarms, hold a mandatory family fire drill. For real. Plan what

everyone needs to do in the event of a fire. Changing the batteries only ensures everyone will know when it's time to panic.

456. Few people get through life without making at least one really bad mistake. The best way to deal with it is to forgive yourself and then do something biblical. Atone.

457. Understand that there are reasons why "Silence is golden" is one of our most popular sayings. Yes, it's time someone offered a yap app.

Colorful Days Diary

For the good of humanity, it's time someone conceived a yap app to monitor the exact number of words each of us speaks in conversation.

Like a helpful exercise pedometer, it would count word-by-word just how much each of us feels compelled to say.

If, for instance, we were in a lunch conversation with three other people, it would vibrate whenever our chat started to race ahead that of our table mates.

The alarms would then increase in severity whenever our word count began to outrun the others' by more than five hundred words per person. Each yap app would include tinker-proof factory settings that would result in self-incineration anytime the device detected that the sound of our voices was making everyone else in the vicinity sick.

Studies about how many words each of us speaks are all over the map. Most say that the average talker speaks about sixteen thousand words a day and that women out-speak men.

The numbers seem flawed. I know some men who can speak sixteen thousand words when ordering a two-item pizza. Worse, they do it like they want the pizza joint to hear them through the window in a thunderstorm from two miles away.

Certainly, many women can talk the ears off acres of corn. They go into excruciating detail about pointless minutia—and it's even worse when it's just women talking to other women.

That's why I advocate in any group of three or more women gathering in public, at least one man should be stationed among the group, sort of like a prison guard assigned to prevent a road gang from malicious conniving.

About 75 percent of what the average woman wants to spout to other women is justifiably hateful things about the average man. But women have a natural and charming shyness about saying it in front of the offending gender.

That applies universally to females, unless you get them all gassed up. Then all bets are off.

Men have no such dainty restrictions regarding what they think is fit to say out loud. Nothing short of ballistic intervention can silence a man determined to talk.

I think most of us talk too much, myself included, because we're desperate to be liked. We think the more we talk the better our chances are of being likable.

In fact, the exact opposite is true.

I've always been drawn to quiet people. Many of my best friends have always been quiet in comparison to your average guy.

And by "quiet," I'm including numerous chums who'll spend consecutive hours passed out cold with their heads seemingly glued to the bar surface. In fact, I prefer the company of the comatose to that of most men who are able to decide—enough's enough—and get up and walk away.

Why do you think I started blogging?

Certainly, deploying the yap app in their company would lead to my ultimate demise.

That's why it's so vital.

The world is absolutely awash in unnecessary words, and most of us are unaware of our contributions.

Just think how much more serene it would be if everyone made a conscious decision to simply reduce the number of words we use.

We'd have more time to think, to enjoy the sounds of nature and proper music. What little we'd have to say would make so much more sense because we'd have thought it through instead of simply unleashing it on ears that are forever struggling to sift knowledge from nonsense.

Imagine the quiet dividend we'd enjoy if all the men and women paid to talk politics were at the mercy of a yap app? Many of the largest offenders would be reduced to silent and sizable piles of ash.

It'd be sublime.

I think I'll stop now before anyone thinks to apply the wise precepts of the yap app to blogging verbosity.

I wouldn't want my family to walk in and discover I've made an ash of myself simply by saying too much.

458. Refer to grocery store clerks who are overly generous with inefficient and wasteful plastic sacks as being "bagnanimous."

459. Remember, honesty without tact is like brain surgery without anesthesia. The operation could cure, but the complications can kill.

460. Colorful conversation starter: Point out to friends that a kid napping is one of the world's most joyful occasions, while a kidnapping is one of the worst. Then exalt, "Behold the power of the space bar!"

461. Warn people who are unreasonable about their fears of new technology that they risk winding up in iPadded cells.

462. Try to convince people that if the institution cared at all about titular accuracy, then fabled Scotland Yard should be called London Building.

463. Construct a clean joke about a mule farmer and a crazy rabbit for the following punch line: "And that's what happened when the farmer got a wild hare up his ass."

464. Tell people who are interested in reincarnation that in your next life you want to come back as a pot just so you can, without being hypocritical, call the kettle black.

465. Be so patient that one day you can boast that you've actually watched a pot boil.

466. Put "Run the Rocky Steps in Philadelphia" on your bucket list and encourage others to do the same. Magical things happen there.

Colorful Days Diary

I'm in a Philadelphia hotel full of romance novelists, and the only stranger who's inspiring any real love is a seventy-something nun.

Good thing I'm not on the make.

More than seven hundred romance novelists are nothing like you'd expect, that is if you'd expect romance novelists are like the vixens on the titillating covers of the bodice rippers they all pen.

They seem homely, fatigued, and talk endlessly in elevators about how clever each of them is.

In short, they're a lot like me, only with successful careers in the writing field.

I love coming to Philadelphia for reasons the romance novelists try to inspire.

My top two man crushes will live forever in Philadelphia.

The first, of course, is Benjamin Franklin, a man so cool it's a confounding surprise to learn he didn't invent sunglasses.

He's the Founding Father whose conceptual fingerprints are today on everything from the way Americans deliver mail (hang in there, USPS!), heat homes, fight community fires, patronize libraries, and, not incidentally, lead and inspire a world—a world that before Franklin was uniformly ruled by monarchs, chieftains, and spiritual pooh-bahs who wielded power based on an alchemic brew of birthright and superstition.

But to me, his greatest invention often goes unmentioned.

Ben Franklin invented America.

He's the spark that ignited the flame that became the American spirit. He's can-do and no quit. He's self-made and selfless. He's free speech and free hors d'oeuvres. Pulitzer Prize-winning biographer

Stacy Schiff describes him as "equal parts Franklin Delano Roosevelt, Ronald Reagan, and Bugs Bunny."

My other love is for the fighter who by one sacrilegious standard is the greatest fighter in history. Sure, Muhammad Ali beat Joe Frazier, but Rocky Balboa, Philadelphia's underdog everyman, is on some scorecards kicking the butt of Franklin, the historical heavyweight.

"To many people, Rocky Balboa has become the identity of Philadelphia," says Meryl Levitz, president of the Greater Philadelphia Tourism Marketing Corporation.

The essence of that can be found at the top of the seventy-two steps at the magnificent Philadelphia Museum of Art where the strains of "Gonna Fly Now" still reverberate. Running the Rocky Steps is one of the history-rich city's biggest tourist attractions. Books have been written about what it means to people who scale the steps.

My daughter and I did on Thursday. We ran clear to the top and then duked it out on the spot where Rocky does his exuberant dance.

The ten-year-old disputes the result, but I contend the scorecards have me kicking her butt.

That was far from the best butt-kicking story told near the Rocky statue that day.

That would be the nun.

The Rocky statue is in a little park-like area just off the foot of the steps. There was a line of people about twenty deep waiting to take their pictures in front of the statue.

There were old and young, tattooed and reserved, the whole human panoply.

Still, the nun with the tripod stood out.

She was in line behind us. We didn't even know she was there until we'd snapped our pictures.

As we walked away, we saw her set up a tripod; she was all alone.

We turned to soak in more of the joyful atmosphere.

She took more than her allotted time, but who has the gall to hustle a nun?

Finally, this frail, slight woman stood before the iconic statue and raised her hands in triumph.

She yelled, "I beat cancer this year, and this picture is going to be on the front of all my Christmas cards!"

And that's the abbreviated story of the nun who loved Rocky.

Think you can beat that one, you published honeys of the romance novel world?

Go ahead and take your best shot.

467. Understand that anytime a cable channel decides to run a Rocky movie marathon, Sylvester Stallone is bound to be yo!-biquitous.

468. The only way anyone's going to want to hear you complain about your financial misfortunes is if you preface the conversation by saying your bottom line has been in dire straits for so long it's surprising it hasn't played bass for Mark Knopfler.

469. Proper or not, some Latin words have corrupted meanings. There's nothing hospitable about hospitals. Colorful people will help correct the problem by referring to them as docitals or discomfitals.

470. Don't complain the next time someone does or says something that throws a real monkey wrench into an already difficult situation. Instead, do something constructive and try to find a loose monkey.

471. Order something in your regular restaurant you've never considered before. If it's good, you'll have a new favorite and an expanded menu option. If it's not, then you'll appreciate your favorites even more.

472. Understand that swearing off profanity might be inherently counterintuitive.

473. Be so pro-organic that you become suspicious anytime you spy a margarine-colored butterfly.

474. Go ahead and describe even sweet-tempered bakers in pie shops as either crusty or flaky.

475. Studies show that thinking about taking a nap is sometimes as refreshing as taking an actual nap. Try to conjure the same sort of magic for things like happy hours.

476. Keep the to-do lists reasonable. Putting ambitious lists together for seven days is bound to make you week-minded.

477. Be alert for rural news stories that will allow you to point out that perverted sheep farmers spend too much time on the lamb.

478. Never accept as factual the statement that time flies. It most certainly does not. Time drives a Maserati down the Autobahn drunk and oblivious to the brick strapped to the accelerator.

479. Become familiar with the catalog of legendary blues master Buddy Guy. The music is soulful, and who wouldn't want to be familiar with a Buddy Guy? It's one of the greatest names in history.

480. Be sympathetic whenever someone complains about the rigors of an upcoming colonoscopy without saying, "Bummer."

481. Colorful conversation starter: note that the Simon & Garfunkel song, "The Sound of Silence," is three minutes and four seconds of titular contradiction.

482. Try to figure out if the change from incandescent to compact fluorescent bulbs will have any effect on the duration of light-years.

483. Many people would prefer to be described as cool, rather than cold, but it's socially acceptable to be warm while appearing hot. It's very mercurial.

484. Be like Barnum. Showman extraordinaire P. T. Barnum was presented with a "gift" of a large tract of land known as "Ivy Island." It was supposed to be an extraordinary gift, and the boy dreamed of the day when he could possess it. Later, he found out it was all a hoax. Still, Barnum used the imaginary land as collateral in a phony investment that earned enough real money to launch his career. Lesson: sometimes imagination means more than money.

485. Get ready for a day in the near future when all the kids will think it's quaint when you tell them you remember when TVs had just one thousand channels.

486. Explain to geography buffs that Rhode Island isn't even Rhode Isthmus.

487. Calculate the actual worth of the organ anytime someone declares Grandma has a "heart of gold." For example, in August 2011, a heart of gold would have been worth $16,978. Something to consider before filling out those organ donor cards.

488. Ask the waitress if the bread sticks fell from bread trees.

489. Contend with a straight face to geography buffs that the Libyan suburbs of Tripoli are Singoli and Douboli.

490. Colorful conversation starter: report to friends on cold days that you saw a man wearing nothing but a musical bellows and he was dressed accordioningly.

491. Aspire to be like the Great Plains Indians of yesteryear. Need little, waste none.

Colorful Days Diary

I shall treat the giant oak that crashed on our property the way Native Americans used to treat the revered buffalo.

I shall respectfully use every bit of it.

When it fell Monday, it sounded like a barrage of firecrackers. But when I strode into the woods to investigate, I saw it wasn't mischievous kids.

I saw what seemed to me a gift from the great Earth God.

I'm disposed to speaking like a proud Native American lately because I'm in the middle of Nathaniel Philbrick's *The Last Stand: Custer, Sitting Bull & Little Bighorn*. Philbrick portrays the Gen. George Armstrong Custer as an ill-advised preening egotist who'd do or say anything to get his name in the headlines, sort of like Trump with better hair.

But the Indians, as they always do, come across as noble victims of cruel palefaces intent on their extermination to quench rapacious land needs.

Before the arrival of my ancestors, the Indians lived mostly at peace upon the land. They wanted not for material goods, and they dealt fairly with the peoples they encountered.

I'm guessing the part where reservation casino patrons complain about rigged slot machines is toward the end.

They had all they needed.

They had the buffalo. Philbrick writes that each Indian consumed about six buffalo a year.

Six! The average buffalo weighs nearly a ton. I can only guess that meant the average Indian weighed something like 825 pounds.

And when I say consumed, I mean consumed.

There was neither horn nor hair left when the Indians were done harvesting the big shaggy.

Check it out:

- Hide uses included moccasins, cradles, sheets, shirts, pipe bags, dolls, and teepees.
- Hair was used for pillows, rope, saddle pads, headdresses, and medicine balls.
- The tails became fly brushes, whips, and decorations.
- The hooves and feet were made into glue and rattles.
- The rawhide uses included shields, lances, drums, pouches, boats, buckets, and rope.
- Trumpet-like horns were made into cups, toys, spoons, ladles, and trumpet-like horns.

And every single morsel of meat was devoured.

It makes me wonder how resourceful squaws responded during each and every meal for their entire lives whenever the family said, "C'mon, not buffalo again!"

An eighteenth-century Great Plains entrepreneur selling pepperoni pizza by the slice would have made a fortune, although it seems likely he'd have been paid in buffalo skin currency, so the point may be moot.

Now, I can't do with a hundred-foot dead tree all the Indians did with a buffalo, although there have been times in my career when things were so bad I've thought about boiling tree bark for breakfast.

But the tree's now grounded canopy—and two others it took out with it—will for a while make a dandy playground for the family.

The creek had eroded the root system, and the top-heavy tree split about fifteen feet up, leaving two splintered sides upright like football goal posts.

The massive trunk now bridges fifty feet of the creek about twenty feet high. I scampered out in the middle of the barked bridge for Val to snap a keeper picture of an ax-wielding me looking like a real he-man.

The picture's composition is weak and looks hurried because I had to cut the photo session short when my fear of heights had me nearly wetting my pants.

That won't matter as I bit-by-bit chainsaw the bounty to use for firewood to warm my loved ones as the winter storms batter the house. I intend to save a gnarly section to polish into a ceremonial mantle for the living room.

Like the Indians whose distant culture still holds me in its compelling thrall, I shall want for nothing.

I shall be at peace with myself and all who share my existence.

That is unless the great Earth God snaps a tree across the TV cable feeding the house with nearly one thousand channels of hi-def entertainment.

Then the family and I will have to turn nomadic for at least until Comcast comes for repairs.

We'll roam the countryside like the Indians of old I so admire.

Where our tribe winds up, who knows?

I hear Buffalo has lots to offer.

492. Exaggerate for more colorful language. For example: "That guy's so old he killed the Dead Sea."

493. Remember, we are all born free and spend the rest of our lives constructing prisons around ourselves. Be sure to, in addition to all that hard-earned security, allow yourself a little built-in liberty.

494. Understand as you go through life that the people who are often most difficult to love are the ones who need love most.

495. Always try to find time to help people who are helping people. Always.

496. Stop wasting your time trying in vain to teach indifferent kids how to live right. Live right and let them watch.

497. Make taking the high road such a habit that confused strangers along the way ask you for directions.

498. Enjoy being human and enjoy human beings.

499. Almost forgot—*Use All the Crayons!* Colorful people everywhere swear it's the key to making your every picture prettier.

500. Once more with feeling: Play! Tickle! Cuddle! Kiss! Hug!

501. Learn the fine art of knowing precisely when to quit.

Acknowledgments

If you've taken the time to read this far or are thumbing through the book and considering a purchase, first of all, thank you. I understand how busy you are, and I appreciate your time. You may have noticed busy is one thing I am not. I have a lot of time on my hands, time to sit around and think about what would happen if a knight in shining armor tried to get through the metal detectors at the airport security gates (see tip no. 34). So *Use All the Crayons!* is sort of like an extended job interview with you and the American public.

See, I'd like to work, but I admit I'm a little picky. I'm seeking a job that includes the word "guru" somewhere in the title. "Nap Guru" probably doesn't pay that much; probably not much demand for a "Bar Guru"; and as fun as "Goo Guru" sounds, it would probably involve showing up to work in a HazMat duds. So I'm thinking "Happiness Guru."

Whether or not that works out remains to be seen, but I'd be remiss, not to mention rude, if I didn't conclude a book about being happy by not thanking the many who through the years have done so much to make me happy.

I'll start with Valerie, Josie, and Lucy; my mother, my late father, my brother and his boys, Brad and Matt; all my cousins and their loved ones; Arnold Palmer, Doc Giffin, and everyone at Arnold Palmer Enterprises. I'd like to thank Dick and Dave Carfang, Keith Ankney, and the whole happy gang at The Pond; Allan Zullo; Barbara M. Neill and The Latrobe Bulletin; Jodi Anne Steiner for encouragement and keen editorial insights; Jeevan Sivasubramaniam at Berrett-Koehler Publishers; Ben Hudson, Kathi Wittkamper, Meredith Lefkoff, and Andrea Long at iUniverse; my fine and feisty readers at www.EightDaysToAmish.com, and all my many other friends from all over the world. Money can't buy happiness or friends like all you guys.

About the Author

Chris Rodell is a Latrobe, Pennsylvania–based writer who has taught creative nonfiction at Point Park University in Pittsburgh. He writes offbeat travel features for msnbc.com and has written features and essays for Esquire, Cooking Light, People, Maxim, Men's Health, Playboy, Golf, Details, and Arnold Palmer's Kingdom magazine. He is the timeline curator for www.ArnoldPalmer.com and blogs at www.EightDaysToAmish.com. He has written for many of the most prestigious magazines in America and been rejected by the rest. He will write for anyone who'll pay him. He is a PROSEtitute.

CPSIA information can be obtained
at www.ICGtesting.com
Printed in the USA
FSHW010055080120
65858FS